Cover: An old Polar Eskimo hunter wears a hood of warm fox fur—ideal protective headgear against the brutal arctic cold. In the background photograph, an Eskimo settlement in the Thule district is whipped by winds during a storm.

Front end-paper: The circle drawn on this outline map of the world encompasses the territory that is the home of the Polar Eskimos—the northernmost people on Earth. They inhabit a thin coastal strip of north-west Greenland that is ice-bound for nine months of each year.

Peoples of the Wild Series

This volume is one in a series that undertakes to record the unique lifestyles of remote peoples who have not yet yielded to the encroaching pressures of the modern world.

PEOPLES OF THE WILD
THE EPIC OF FLIGHT
THE SEAFARERS
WORLD WAR II
THE GOOD COOK
THE TIME LIFE ENCYCLOPAEDIA OF GARDENING
HUMAN BEHAVIOUR
THE GREAT CITIES
THE ART OF SEWING
THE OLD WEST
THE WORLD'S WILD PLACES
THE EMERGENCE OF MAN
LIFE LIBRARY OF PHOTOGRAPHY
THIS FABULOUS CENTURY
TIME-LIFE LIBRARY OF ART
FOODS OF THE WORLD
GREAT AGES OF MAN
LIFE SCIENCE LIBRARY
LIFE NATURE LIBRARY
YOUNG READERS LIBRARY
LIFE WORLD LIBRARY
THE TIME-LIFE BOOK OF BOATING
TECHNIQUES OF PHOTOGRAPHY
LIFE AT WAR
LIFE GOES TO THE MOVIES
BEST OF LIFE

Hunters of the Polar North

The Eskimos

by Wally Herbert
and the Editors of Time-Life Books
Photographs by Bryan Alexander

PEOPLES OF THE WILD · TIME-LIFE BOOKS · AMSTERDAM

Published by Time-Life Books B.V., Ottho Heldringstraat 5, 1066 AZ Amsterdam.

ISBN 7054 0701 2

Contents

The Author
A distinguished polar explorer and author, Wally Herbert has travelled more than 25,000 miles in the Arctic and Antarctic regions by dog sledge and in open boats. Much of this distance has been traversed in pioneering journeys: he has mapped some 46,000 square miles of previously uncharted territory in the Antarctic and in 1969, with three companions, he completed the first surface crossing of the Arctic Ocean. He has spent a total of 14 years in the polar regions, including four winters with the Polar Eskimos.

The Photographer
Bryan Alexander is an award-winning photojournalist whose work has appeared in publications in 36 countries. His special field of interest is the far north: in addition to Greenland, he has covered Lapland, and the arctic regions of Canada and the U.S.S.R. He first visited the Polar Eskimos in 1971, travelling on a scholarship awarded by Britain's Royal Society of the Arts. The photographs for this volume were taken on his third trip to Greenland.

The Volume Consultants
Rolf Gilberg inherited an interest in the Polar Eskimos from his parents, who lived for a year in north-west Greenland, where his father worked as a doctor. A graduate of the University of Copenhagen, he has worked since 1971 as curator of the Department of Ethnography in the National Museum of Denmark. He has made three field-study trips to north-west Greenland, and has published more than 20 articles and papers on the Polar Eskimos.

A Reader in Arctic Studies at Cambridge University, Dr. Terence Armstrong is also the assistant director of the University's Scott Polar Research Institute. Among his many books are *The Northern Sea Route*, *The Russians in the Arctic*, and—with B. B. Roberts and C. W. M. Swithinbank—*An Illustrated Glossary of Snow and Ice*.

Dr. Regitze Søby is a lecturer and research fellow at the Institute of Eskimology of the University of Copenhagen, and the author of several monographs on the Polar Eskimos. Her special field of study is the social condition of the settlements of northern Greenland, where she has spent more than four years engaged in field work.

The Series Consultant
Malcolm McLeod, Keeper of Ethnography at the British Museum, was born in Edinburgh. After studying History and Social Anthropology at Oxford, he undertook research in Africa, concentrating on the Asante region and other areas of Ghana. He has taught in the Sociology Department of the University of Ghana and at Cambridge, and is the author of a book on the Asante.

Introduction

The land of the Eskimos spans national frontiers and even continents, but everywhere it is bounded by snow and ice. The people inhabit arctic wastes that stretch from eastern Siberia through Alaska and Canada to Greenland—perhaps the harshest environment to which human beings have adapted. Ever since the 10th century, when Viking explorers first chronicled their existence, stories of the Eskimos' struggle for survival have gripped the imagination of dwellers in more temperate lands. Today, there are still Eskimo groups scattered across the arctic regions who share a common language and physiognomy. But the modern world has encroached upon them and few live as their ancestors did.

So, when Time-Life Books decided to include a volume on the Eskimos in the *Peoples of the Wild* series, the first task was to find a group that adhered to its traditional culture. Attention soon focused on the Eskimos of north-west Greenland, who live less than a thousand miles from the North Pole. Their extremely remote location has helped to isolate them from the rest of Greenland as well as from foreign contacts; they still support themselves primarily by hunting, as their forefathers did, and travel by dog sledge.

The next step was to find a writer and a photographer with the skill and stamina necessary to work for several months far above the Arctic Circle. The decision was soon made. Author Wally Herbert and photographer Bryan Alexander were acknowledged arctic experts with prior experience of Polar Eskimo life. They agreed enthusiastically to the assignment.

For 10 months, the two men criss-crossed the Polar Eskimos' territory, sledging with them and sharing their homes. Their mission did not always go smoothly. At one time Alexander was knocked over by a sledge drawn by bolting dogs and seriously injured his eye. He was flown to Denmark for medical treatment, but was back in Greenland in just over a week.

The two men endured arctic gales, white-outs—freak weather conditions in which multiple reflections between an overcast sky and the snow blot the landscape from view—and dangerous sledge journeys over breaking sea-ice. But they also enjoyed the warmth of Polar Eskimo hospitality and became linked by deep bonds of friendship to their hosts. When they returned to England, they were able to draw on all their wide knowledge of north-west Greenland to prepare this volume, which was then checked with the help of an international team of consultants. As you will discover, this book stands as a personal testament to the respect and affection both men feel for a small, hardy group of people living, much as they have done from time immemorial, at the northernmost limits of the inhabited world.

The Editors

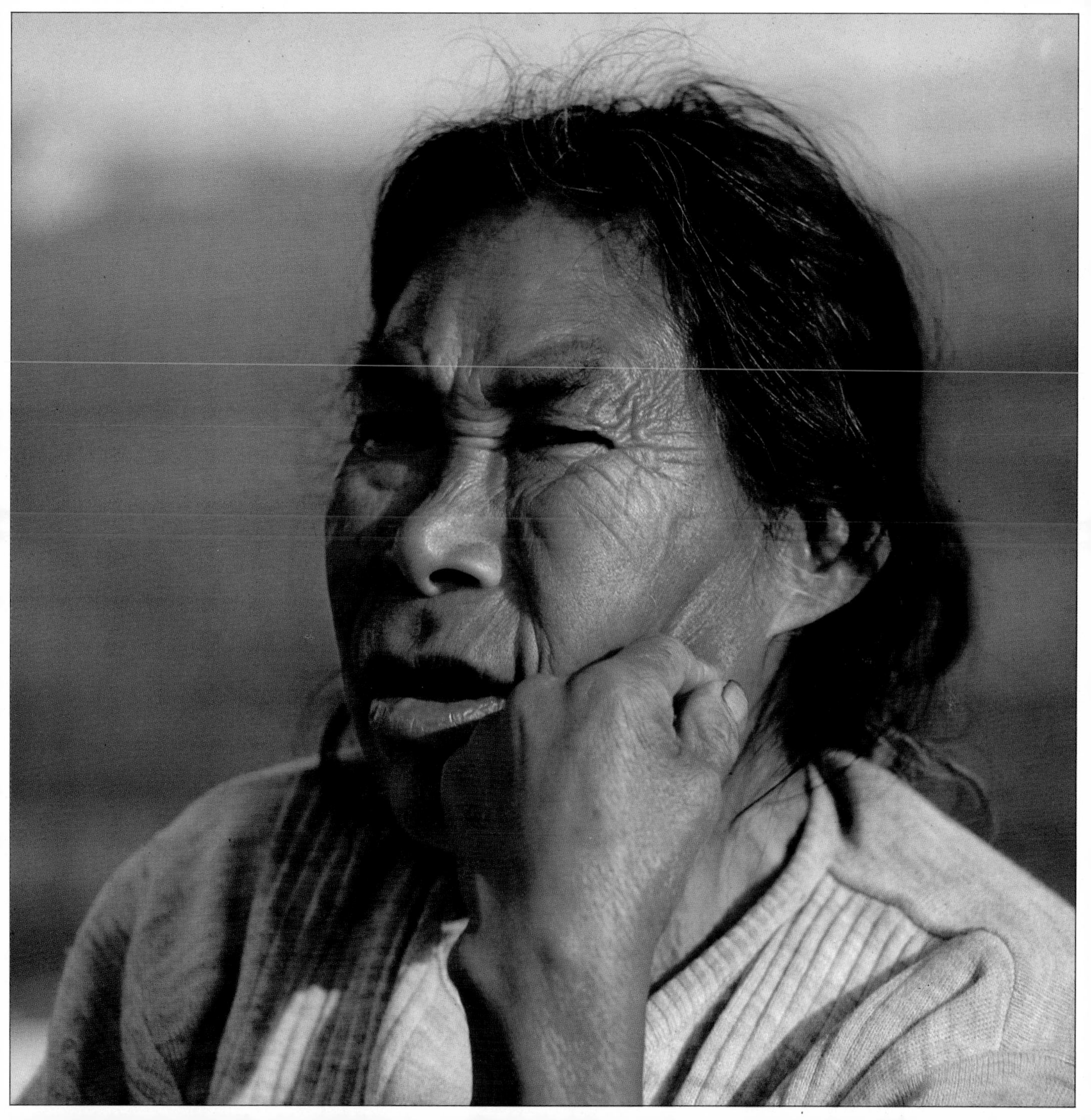

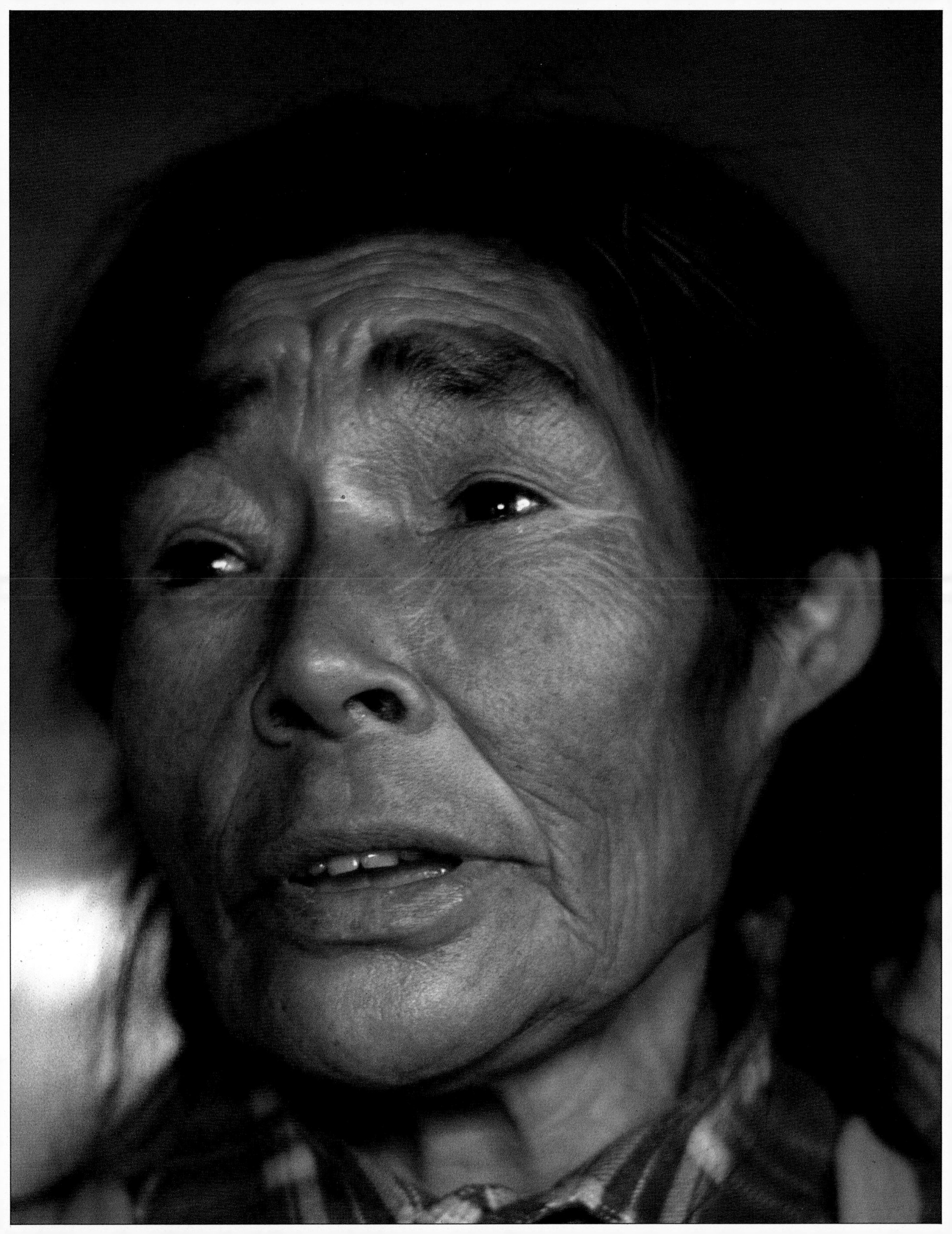

One | At Home North of the World

Among the persisting memories of my first visit to the village of Siorapaluk in 1966, one in particular has always affected me deeply. I had merely taken one step beyond the northern limits of the village and then turned to gaze idly over the frozen waters of the fiord on which it lies. It did not occur to me for some moments that there was anything significant in what I had done. But then, suddenly, I realized that in taking that single step I had placed myself north of every native man, woman and child on the face of the Earth. I have seldom experienced such a glorious feeling of pride.

Since that day I have travelled farther north, to the Pole itself, and the delight I experienced in Siorapaluk now strikes me as somewhat naive. Yet hidden within the pride I felt that day lies the essential clue to the survival of the Polar Eskimos. The unique position this extraordinary people occupy as the northernmost community on Earth gives them a sense of being superior to other men. In triumphing over the hardships of their arctic environment—the bitter cold, the frequent exposure to danger and the threat of hunger—the Polar Eskimos believe that they have demonstrated their preeminence over dwellers in more temperate lands, who do not have to face such challenges. Without that conviction, I believe, they would long ago have found themselves on that same downward spiral that all other Eskimo groups began early in the present century.

The region that the Polar Eskimos inhabit is known to Westerners as Thule, a name bestowed on it by the Danish explorer Knud Rasmussen, after the legendary land that the ancient Greeks believed lay at the northernmost limits of the habitable world. The Thule district lies between 75° and 80° latitude on the rugged north-west coast of Greenland. Constitutionally part of Denmark, Greenland is the largest island on Earth, with a deeply indented 24,500-mile coastline—almost equal in total length to the equatorial circum-

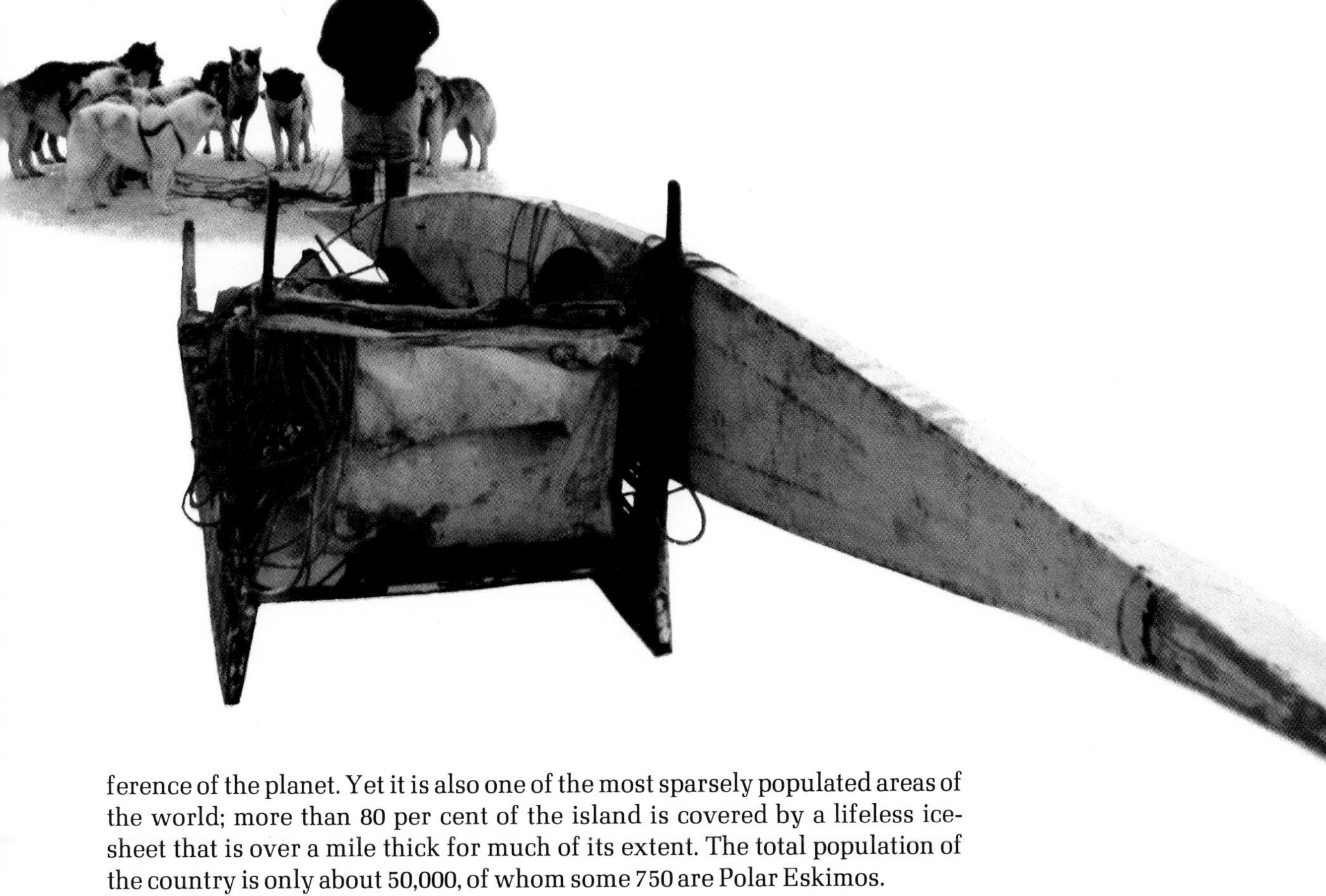

ference of the planet. Yet it is also one of the most sparsely populated areas of the world; more than 80 per cent of the island is covered by a lifeless ice-sheet that is over a mile thick for much of its extent. The total population of the country is only about 50,000, of whom some 750 are Polar Eskimos.

Even by the standards of this vast and desolate island, the Thule region is remote. It is a small oasis of habitable land in a surrounding desert of ice. To visit their nearest neighbours to the south, the Polar Eskimos must make a journey of 400 miles along the uninhabited coastline of Melville Bay. Their territory is bounded to the west by the headwaters of Baffin Bay. Northwards, there is no sign of life between them and the Pole, more than 800 miles away, except for a few archaeological sites along Greenland's north coast—evidence that once, long ago, the territory was less hostile to man than it is today. To the east, the uninhabitable Greenland ice-sheet stretches 600 miles or more. In theory, it is possible for the Polar Eskimos to meet with their fellow-countrymen on the east coast by skirting the ice-sheet's northern edge; but to do so they would have to embark on a hazardous 2,500-mile journey that I myself attempted with one companion in 1978 and that I can testify passes through barren wastelands for most of the way.

My burgeoning interest in arctic exploration had originally brought me to the district. At the time of my first visit to Siorapaluk, I was outward bound with two companions on a 1,500-mile journey to retrace the route of the pioneer explorer Dr. Frederick Cook, a controversial figure whom we believed to have been the first man to reach the North Pole, in 1908. We had chosen his route as training for a more ambitious expedition across the longest axis of the Arctic Ocean by way of the Pole, to be mounted the following year.

I still recall with amusement and embarrassment the affectionate concern shown to us by the Eskimos with whom we wintered. None of them believed we would succeed, and several even marked crosses on our maps to indicate the exact position where they predicted we would perish. All three of us were experienced polar travellers, with a combined total of 14 winters in the Antarctic and the Arctic, and many thousands of miles' journeying across unexplored country; but I could see in the eyes of our hosts the projected image of three over-eager young men going blindly to their deaths.

We did successfully complete the journey and duly returned to Thule the following winter, where we enjoyed the pleasures of a friendly reunion with our surprised Eskimo friends. Since then I have returned to the region many times and, in the course of these visits, the Thule district has become almost a second home to me. The more I learn about the hardy people who inhabit it, the greater is the respect I hold for them.

The territory that the Polar Eskimos inhabit confounds all the expectations of uninformed visitors from the south. To begin with, the characteristics of its seasons differ more radically than anything experienced in temperate lands. Each winter, from late October to February, the Polar Eskimos experience four months of permanent darkness while the Earth is tilted away from the sun. Correspondingly in summer, from mid-April until August, they are compensated with four months of continuous daylight when the sun is north of the equator. Only in the intermediate periods—the spring and autumn—do the Polar Eskimos enjoy the alternation of light and darkness within a 24-hour span that most of the world takes for granted.

It is impossible for any non-Eskimo, accustomed to a diurnal balance of night and day, to appreciate the sensation of the four-month polar night; the fear of continuous darkness felt by men of temperate latitudes is primeval in its origins and almost inconsolable. Yet, to the Eskimos and those few explorers who have spent several years in the polar regions within 15° latitude of the North or South Poles, the long night is a magical period. Although there is no sunlight, the darkness is far from total. The light of the moon and the stars is not only reflected but magnified by the enveloping snow and ice, contradicting the very concept of darkness and lightening the heart.

Nor is the four-month period of daylight a tedious compensation for a winter without sun. The biological clock of the Eskimos, and of some of the longer-term polar explorers, tends to readjust. The temperature rises to a midsummer average of 41°F and, since there is no nightfall to regulate its working, the body is freed to find its natural rhythm. The Eskimos sleep when they want, while the plants grow intensively and the wildlife multiplies to restore the food supply. As for the short spring and autumn periods, in which the sun both rises and sets each day, these two transitional seasons provide the wedge of twilight between light and darkness, and this gives the Eskimos time again to get used to the presence or absence of light.

The Polar Eskimos, then, have come to terms with the seasons of their year; but none of them would be too proud to deny that their effects, combined with those of their district's extreme northern latitudes, have been to create an environment less friendly to man than that of almost any other part

A glacier gravitates inexorably towards the sea from its source high on the Greenland ice-sheet, a frozen mantle as much as 10,000 feet thick. North-west Greenland's glaciers move at the rate of about 50 yards a year and spawn some 40,000 icebergs annually.

of the Earth. To visitors from the south, the most obvious hardship the Polar Eskimos have to endure is the cold. The average temperature during the winter months is –22°F. That figure may come as a mild surprise; there are many millions of people elsewhere on Earth who have experienced lower temperatures. But not as a sustained condition of life. The worker who travels to his office in a heated car from a comfortable, centrally heated home can have no possible conception of the effect of the cold on a Polar Eskimo who is exposed to the elements for as much as 15 hours a day, sometimes for weeks or even months on end. The effect on the body of a 40-knot wind when the air temperature is a tolerable –30°F presents an equivalent chill factor of –100°F, and winds of more than 100 knots occur frequently in this part of the Arctic at certain times of the year.

The Polar Eskimos are well prepared by nature to face the harshness of their environment. Like all the other Eskimo peoples scattered through the Arctic between eastern Siberia and Greenland, they are short in stature and stockily built, adaptations that help to reduce the rate at which the body loses heat. Layers of fat that, over the generations, have accumulated over exposed parts of their bodies—cheeks, eyelids, hands and feet—also cut down heat loss, aiding survival in the sub-zero temperatures of the winter months. Each individual develops further protection against the extreme environment during his life. Adult Eskimos have an unusually dense network of veins and arteries in their fingers and toes that serves to combat the cold by providing an increased blood flow. In addition, their powers of sight and hearing often greatly exceed those of other peoples. When their eyesight was tested by a Danish optician, some Eskimos proved capable of deciphering even the smallest print on the standard optical card from twice the distance at which it is normally presented, giving them in effect 200 per cent vision.

Temperamentally the Polar Eskimos are equally well attuned to the world in which they live. They are natural stoics, who instinctively impose a tight discipline upon their actions and emotions. Though they react quickly when circumstances demand it, their self-control in moments of real danger—on breaking sea-ice, say, in the middle of a storm—is wonderful to behold.

The obverse of this tight mental discipline is the raucous humour that is one of their most endearing characteristics. An irrepressible sense of fun will burst out at the most solemn moments, expressing itself in practical jokes and slapstick of every kind. As an Eskimo bends over, intent on some minor chore, a friend will creep up behind him and seize him by the calf, revelling in his victim's momentary panic as he thinks a rogue dog has him in its jaws. A young man will climb a sloping iceberg, then fold himself into a ball and roll down, head over heels, shooting far out on to the ice at its foot while his companions clutch their sides in glee.

Over the centuries, physical and mental alertness have been vital to the Polar Eskimos since they have depended for their continued survival solely on their hunting skills. No vegetation can grow in the Thule district during the winter, and even in the summer months the Polar Eskimos have never raised crops. Traditionally, they have lived exclusively off the game they kill, and even today, when they have access to many imported foodstuffs from Denmark, their way of life is still based on hunting.

Considering its latitude, the district is amazingly prolific in wildlife. The principal food sources are seal and walrus, which are hunted throughout the year. The arctic hares that inhabit the valleys running down from the ice-sheet are a secondary, but similarly perennial, food resource. The foxes with whom the hares share this habitat provide fur for clothing. The Eskimos' most feared and prized prey, the polar bear, leads a nomadic life, wandering far over the sea-ice, where it is hunted partly for its meat but especially for its fur. In the summer, the region's cliffs and coastal hills teem with birdlife of almost every arctic species; eider ducks, gulls, geese, terns, fulmars and, most important, little auks, which flock to the Thule district in millions and provide a particularly prized delicacy. When the ice melts, there are fish to catch, notably polar cod and arctic char. Although the larger whales, once found here in great numbers, are seldom seen these days, the smaller arctic whales—such as the narwhal and the distinctively coloured beluga, or white whale—are regular visitors to the district's fiords.

Like most successful predators, the Polar Eskimos rely on mobility to track down their prey. Their principal means of transport is the dog sledge, and no other northern peoples can match their skill in handling the dog teams. The territory they range over in sledges is vast. The distance from Siorapaluk, in the north, to the southernmost settlement, Savigsivik, is not much more than 150 miles as the raven flies; but because of the nature of the terrain, travel in the Thule district has little to do with the logic of straight lines, so the real distance by sledge amounts to more than double that span. Yet the well-marked trails from village to village represent only a small fraction of the total area the Polar Eskimos cover.

Here again, the reality of the polar environment confounds conventional expectations. By far the greater part of their hunting territories lies not inland from the coastline—where the ice-sheet, uninhabited and almost devoid of animal life, discourages travel—but out to sea. The frozen waters off their coast provide the Eskimos with rich hunting grounds that vary in their total extent according to the season and the state of the ice. My own calculation is that, in the months of February, March and April, before the summer thaw gets under way, the maximum span available to the hunter is as much as 38,000 square miles. If the few regularly used overland routes over glaciers—used as short cuts around capes and other places where the sea-ice is normally unsafe—are also taken into account, the distances covered by the Polar Eskimos on their sledges stretch the imagination to the breaking-point.

Over the years, much of this vast area has become familiar to me, and there were many places I wanted to revisit when I last returned to the district. I flew into Thule Air Base, a gleaming aggregation of ultra-modern Western technology built in Polar Eskimo territory in the 1950s as part of NATO's air defences. It was night when my plane arrived, the permanent night of the polar winter, but by the light of the stars I could see from the air the thin strip

The Region Called Avanersuup Kommunia

The homeland of the Polar Eskimos lies far within the Arctic Circle in north-west Greenland, facing Baffin Bay (inset map). A deeply indented coastline backed by a vast, barren ice-sheet, it was formally named the Thule District in 1937, when Greenland was a colony of Denmark. After Greenland became self-governing in 1980, the official name of the region was changed to Avanersuup Kommunia, meaning the Commune in the Far North; outside Greenland, however, it is still usually known as the Thule district.

Despite its high latitude, the district has a relatively mild climate, due largely to the warm currents from the south that pass up the east side of Baffin Bay. The sea off the Thule coast never freezes over and its open waters are well stocked with the sea mammals on which the hunters depend. The sheltered fiords and bays remain ice-bound for up to 10 months of the year, however, thereby providing sledging routes to the open sea.

The need for easy access to the sea long ago determined the sites of the Eskimos' villages. Scattered along 350 miles of coast, from the north side of Inglefield Sound to Melville Bay (main map), they nestle in the lee of points and islands. Many of them are also close to glaciers that run down from the ice-sheet and can be used as overland sledging routes.

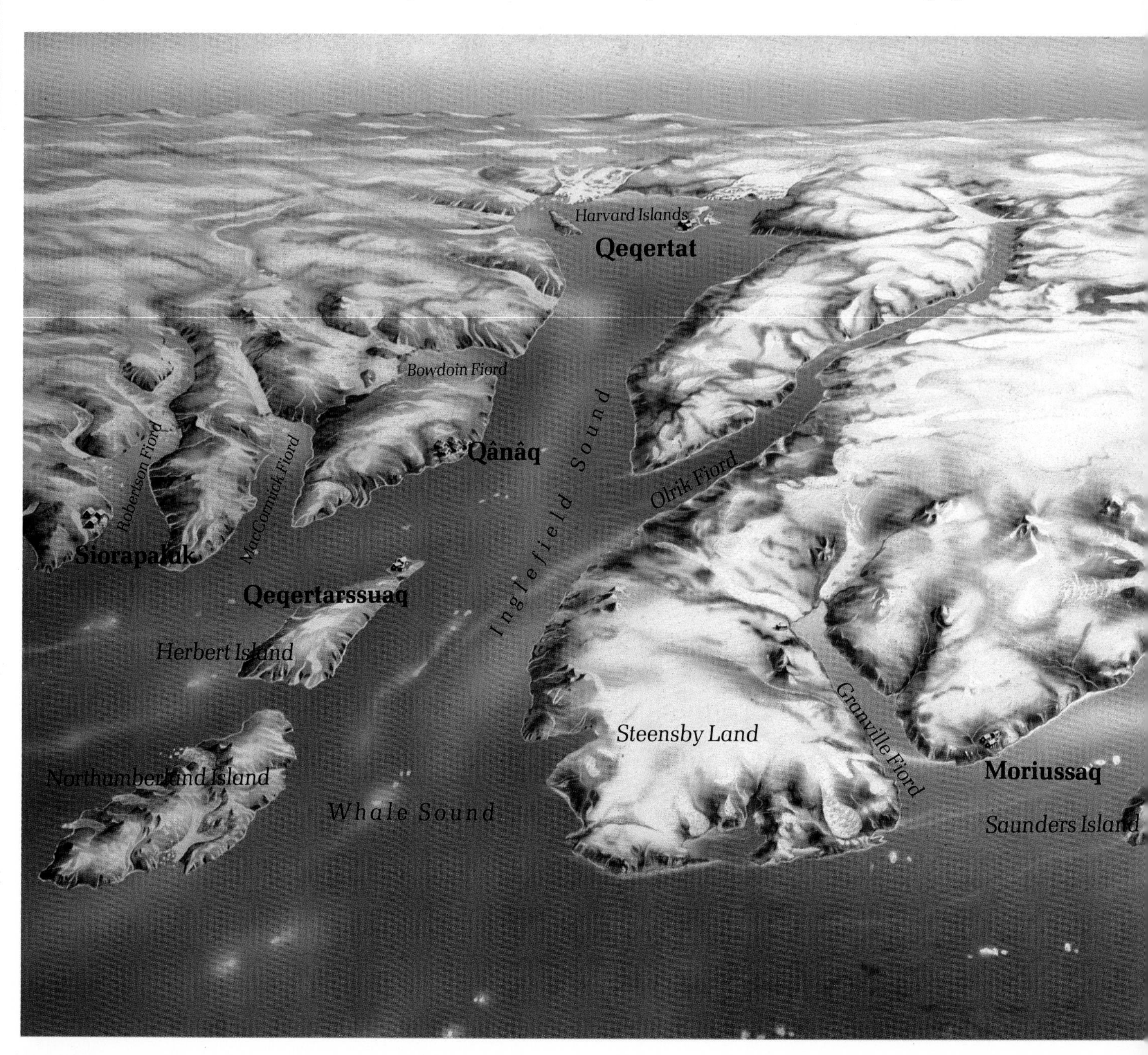

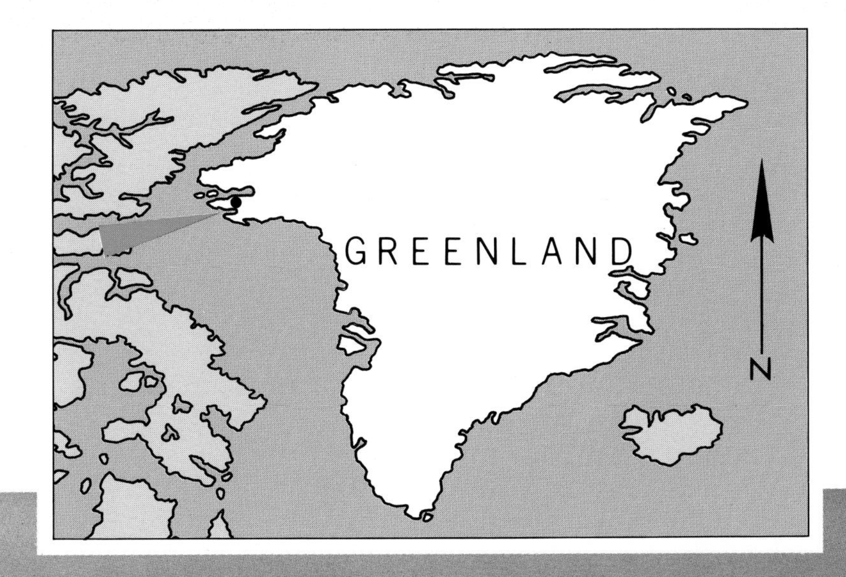

ICE-SHEET

Savigsivik

Cape York

Melville Bay

Crimson Cliffs

Dundas

Thule Air Base

Narssârssuk

Parker Snow Bay

Pitugfik Glacier

Wolstenholme Island

Baffin Bay

of shoreline the Eskimos inhabit, squeezed in between the frozen sea and the featureless ice-sheet we had been flying over for the past two hours.

The air base lies on the southern shore of the 20-mile-long Wolstenholme Fiord which—together with the 55-mile-long Inglefield Sound 50 miles to the north—is one of Thule's two most distinctive geographic features. I was to see a great deal more of both these inlets in the following two months, as I criss-crossed the starkly beautiful arctic wilderness in search of places and faces that I knew from the past.

In the course of those months, I journeyed over much of the Thule district, travelling with the Eskimos' own spontaneity as weather and circumstance dictated. Naturally Siorapaluk was one of my chosen destinations, and on arriving there I found that the very sledge tracks in the snow around that windswept string of dwellings revived warming memories. To the north, there were only two or three sets of tracks, marking the passage of hunters who had ventured out in search of game; but to the south the trail was wide and hard-packed, indicating the busy sledge traffic to and from the village. I enjoyed a happy reunion with those of my friends who still lived in their old homes. I was greeted by hunters I had known for years and had the grey hairs in my beard counted by women I had met as a young man.

On that visit I reached my northern limit at Siorapaluk; thereafter my way lay, with all the other sledges, down the trail southwards towards the settlements lining Inglefield Sound. As a passenger on an Eskimo friend's sledge, I headed back to the eastern of the two islands that dominate the mouth of the fiord. Coincidentally named Herbert Island, it brings back very special memories for me; I once lived there for two years with my wife and daughter while gathering material for a documentary film about the Polar Eskimos. We had stayed in the village of Qeqertarssuaq, a cluster of 13 houses, none of which seemed big enough to house the greatest hunters I had ever known.

In all, there are six permanent settlements in the Thule district besides the air base and its attendant village of Dundas, which is occupied almost exclusively by Danes who work at the base or provide ancillary services for its staff. Two of the settlements are located, like Qeqertarssuaq, on the shores of Inglefield Sound. The tiny village of Qeqertat lies on an island about 50 miles east of Qeqertarssuaq, at the bottom end of the Sound. It is off the beaten track even for the keenest travellers, except in summer when hunters gather there to pursue the schools of narwhal that glide into the inlet to calve.

Much closer to Qeqertarssuaq, on the mainland coast, lies Qânâq, Thule's largest settlement and administrative centre, which is locally referred to as a town, although it has only about 350 inhabitants. Unlike the villages, Qânâq has an electric power plant, and in clear weather during the polar night we had been able to see its lights from our hut, 15 miles away across the ice.

It is a strangely divided place, for it marks the nexus between the hunting culture of the Polar Eskimos and the modern world. It is the home of all the main social facilities of the region, including a small hospital and a boarding-school that Polar Eskimo teenagers attend. Here, too, are the well-built houses of the administrators and technicians from Denmark and southern

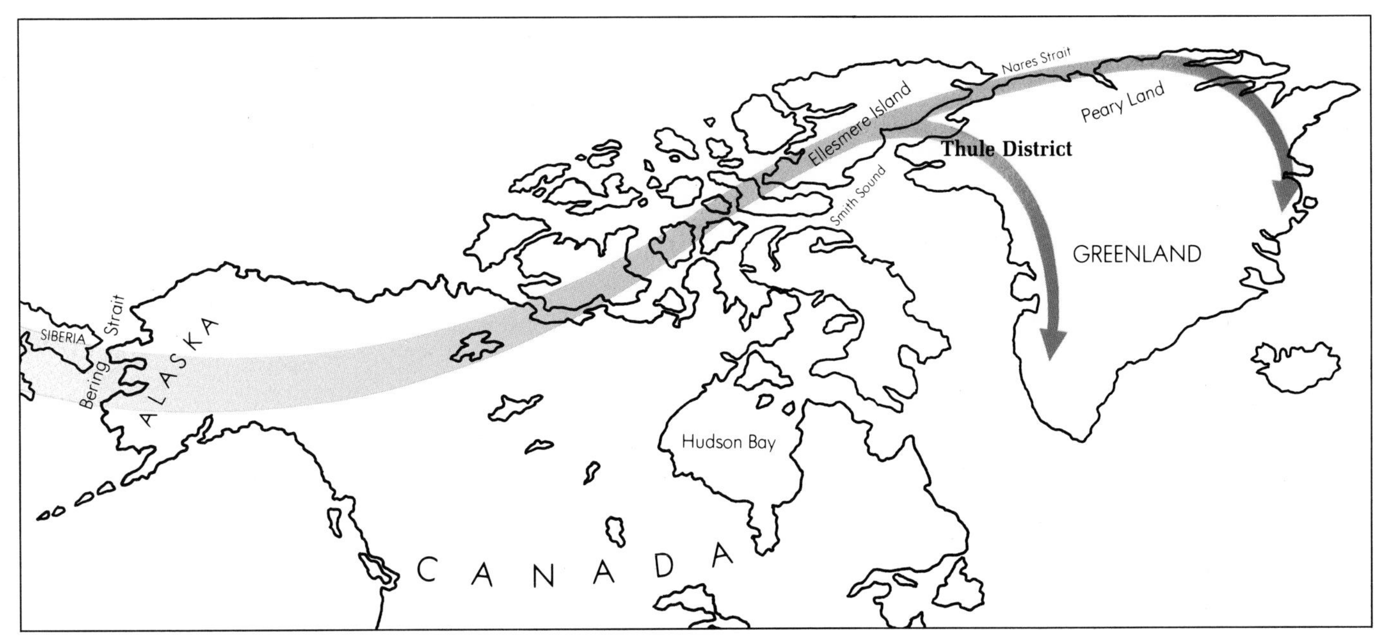

The territory now occupied by the Polar Eskimos was for thousands of years one of the two main gateways to Greenland for Eskimos migrating from the west. From the Bering Strait region, they travelled across arctic Canada to Ellesmere Island. While many crossed Smith Sound to the Thule district to settle there or continue south, others found a passage to Greenland's east coast via the narrow head of Nares Strait and the now desolate lands of the far north.

Greenland—the men in charge of the Greenland Technical Organization, which supervises construction in the district, and of the Royal Greenland Trade Department, which runs the stores where the Eskimos trade skins and furs for money with which to buy essential supplies: hunting equipment, ammunition, household utensils and such foodstuffs as tea, coffee, biscuits and sugar. Some of Qânâq's Eskimo residents—many of them employed by the administration—now also live in solid, modern houses with electricity and running water, comforts that previous generations would never have known or even guessed at. Yet the town always strikes me as an ungainly hybrid, a strange, confused place whose Eskimo residents seem unsure of their new place in the world. I spent little time in Qânâq; I prefer the harsher world of the Polar Eskimos who still follow their traditional way of life.

South of Qânâq, across the fiord's mouth, lies the imposing bulk of Steensby Land, a mountainous outcrop that thrusts like a gigantic muzzle into Baffin Bay. The sledge route from Qânâq to the southern settlements of Moriussaq and Savigsivik ascends a glacier that shines in sunlight as though made of shattered glass and gleaming streams of molten silver, then descends again to the smaller Granville Fiord. I know that fiord well, although on the first occasion that I sledged down it, I did not see it at all. I had set off from Qânâq on a midwinter's journey southwards in the company of Avataq, one of the most skilled hunters of the region. After crossing the glacier and its many hidden perils, the prospect of a smooth trip down the fiord was balm to my nerves. But instead of being an easy run it turned into a nightmare. For 10 hours we drove our two teams of dogs into a blizzard. The wind was too strong to set up our tent, so we were forced to feel our way in pitch darkness along the eastern shore in a desperate effort to reach Moriussaq at the mouth of the fiord; the shelter of the village there was our only hope of survival. The last two miles of the 20-mile journey down the fiord were one of the most frightening experiences of my life. Avataq and I literally crawled those miles on our hands and knees, roped to our dogs and to each other to avoid losing contact in the blinding storm.

When finally we discerned the vague shapes of the village shacks, it was hard to believe they were real until we had actually crawled inside one of them. It turned out that the kind couple who opened their arms and embraced us were celebrated throughout the Thule district. The husband was the great hunter Qâvigarssuaq. Both he and his ebullient wife, Bebiane, are now dead, but Qâvigarssuaq remains a legend among his people. As a young man he had accompanied Knud Rasmussen as a guide and helper on a three-year journey of almost 4,000 miles: from Thule by boat to Hudson Bay, and on from there by dog sledge to Alaska. It was the longest sledging journey ever made across the Canadian Arctic. As a result, Qâvigarssuaq was decorated by the Danish government and received by President Coolidge of the United States. When he returned home, his stories of his travels and descriptions of the places and events he had seen went so far beyond the boundaries of his people's experience as to be almost impossible for his fellow-hunters to comprehend. Yet he was a modest man and, to his last breath, a man more proud of his heritage than of all the honours that had been conferred upon him.

Qâvigarssuaq was my own direct link with Polar Eskimo history. In the years before his death, I spent many hours with him in his Moriussaq home, listening to tales of Eskimo life that often had their roots in the distant past. But the history of the Thule district stretches a long way further back than even the dimmest folk-memory inherited by my friend from his ancestors.

The first travellers to cross Smith Sound, the strait that most closely connects the island chain leading from the Canadian mainland to Thule, arrived in the district more than 4,000 years ago, when the climate was a good deal milder than it is today. At that time there were musk oxen in great numbers at these latitudes. Migrant hunters followed these herds eastwards from Canada into Greenland by two distinct routes. Some travelled to the northern extremity of Ellesmere Island, across the Nares Strait from Greenland, before making the crossing. Then they went to now-uninhabited Peary Land, 500 miles north-east of Thule, where the ruins of a number of settlements have been found, establishing the presence of people there as early as 2,000 B.C. The hunters who took the more southerly route across Smith Sound—a route I myself took in the reverse direction in 1967—settled for a while in the territory now occupied by the Polar Eskimos, where again there is evidence from ancient sites of their presence between 3,000 and 4,000 years ago.

These crossing-points were used by successive waves of Eskimos through to the present millennium. Most of these migrations across the Canadian Arctic, some perhaps from as far afield as the original Eskimo homeland in the Bering Strait regions of Siberia and Alaska, spread out through the island after passing through the transit points in northern Greenland. But one group that crossed over Smith Sound in the late ninth or early 10th century A.D. did not move southwards. Instead, they settled at their point of arrival, attracted, it seems, by the presence of whales in the vicinity. This group constituted the direct ancestors of today's Polar Eskimos.

After the 15th century, the climate of the polar regions worsened steadily as a result of one of the still unexplained long-term climatic fluctuations that periodically affect the planet. This deterioration, which reached a nadir in the 17th century, had a minimal effect on the temperate lands of the West; but in the Arctic its consequences for the ecology and hunting cultures of the coasts were dramatic. The increase in pack ice closed the regular sea-lanes used by the small Eskimo groups in their migrations eastwards, and a drop of only two or three degrees in the median temperature put the very existence of the Polar Eskimos at risk. The result was to cut the Eskimos off from all contact with their fellow-Greenlanders to the south. During the 18th century, the climate began to ameliorate throughout the Arctic; but it was not until the beginning of the 19th century that the Polar Eskimos were able to renew contact with the outside world.

When contact was re-established, it was not with other Eskimo groups but with European explorers from the south. The name of the Polar Eskimo's discoverer was John Ross. He was a captain in the Royal Navy and at the time of the meeting with the Eskimos he was commanding two ships on an exploratory voyage through Baffin Bay. In 1818, when his expedition was dispatched, the Eskimos as a race were no longer a novelty to the Western world. It was thought, however, that their territories extended no farther than 74° latitude, because of the severity of the climate and the length of the polar night beyond that point. The vast area north of this latitude was considered to be an uninhabited wilderness containing only three features of any possible interest to man: the still undiscovered North-West Passage from the Atlantic Ocean to the Pacific Ocean, the North Pole and, on the other side of the American continent, the North-East Passage.

Ross's goal was to discover the North-West Passage. He failed in this objective, and his unexpected encounter with the Polar Eskimos, at a point thought to be beyond the northernmost limits of human habitation, was his only consolation for an otherwise unsuccessful voyage. The meeting took place on the northern shore of Melville Bay, near Cape York. As the ships stood out from the coast, Ross's men were astonished to see several rudely fashioned dog sledges moving over the inshore ice. Ross at once commanded the ships to put in towards land, hoping to make contact with the sledges' drivers. He had on board a young Eskimo interpreter called John Sacheuse. Sacheuse had grown up in a mission station in southern Greenland, but had run away to sea aboard a Scottish whaling-ship. It was largely through his knowledge of the Eskimo language that contact was finally established.

The first efforts of the Englishmen and Sacheuse to entice the Eskimos met with little success. The drivers fled at their approach. It was not until the following day that a meeting was effected by an offer of gifts. Sacheuse then managed to persuade five Eskimos to venture out to Ross's ship. The vessel

At the first meeting between Polar Eskimos and Europeans, in 1818, the British naval explorers Captain John Ross and Lieutenant Edward Parry (centre) exchange knives for narwhal tusks after landing at Prince Regent's Bay, now Melville Bay. The scene was drawn by John Sacheuse, a southern Greenlander, who included himself in the picture, standing with two Eskimos admiring their reflections in a mirror.

The setting sun gilds the windows of Moriussaq, a village of about 60 people on the northern shore of Wolstenholme Fiord. Near good hunting grounds, Moriussaq is one of the larger Eskimo settlements, with a trading store and school paid for by the Greenland authorities. The small structures adjoining most of the wooden houses are shacks used to store fuel and racks for meat.

was unlike anything the Eskimos could ever have imagined, and one can only admire their courage in boarding it. They seemed convinced that it was a living creature; one addressed it, in evident terror, with cries of: "Who are you? What are you? Where do you come from—the Sun or the Moon?"

Once on board, they found themselves in a totally unfamiliar world, full of strange sights and sounds. They delighted the crew by the sheer incongruity of their reactions and by their total ignorance of the outside world. When a pig—one of several carried on the ship as a source of fresh meat—snorted at them, one Eskimo fled in terror. A watch was held to another Eskimo's ear; supposing it to be alive, he asked if it was good to eat. A third visitor, on being presented with a wine glass, "appeared very much astonished that it did not melt with the heat of his hand," according to Ross's published account of the meeting, "no doubt from an idea he entertained that it was made of ice."

It must be observed that, right to the end of this unexpected and historic meeting, Ross and his men conducted themselves with courtesy and good-humoured kindness. Nothing they said or did was in any way intended to belittle or intimidate their guests. Their five-day visit, nevertheless, broke the spell of isolation for this solitary people, for the Polar Eskimos' existence was finally known to the outside world.

There was no immediate rush of visitors to their territory. Some whalers working off the southern shores of Greenland extended their range northwards to trade with the Eskimos. For explorers, too, Ross's journey had important implications: it suggested that the headwaters of Baffin Bay might offer an opening to the north. As the century drew to an end, interest was focused on the North Pole, for man's dream of reaching that point on the globe where the lines of longitude meet was becoming a passionate obsession.

The contribution of the Polar Eskimos to the exploration of the route to the Pole was immense. Both Dr. Frederick Cook and Commander Robert Peary exploited the Eskimos' knowledge and skills in their pioneering journeys. During the first decade of the new century, at least one-third of the entire male population of the Thule district was directly involved in the quest, but the motivation behind it remained baffling to the Eskimos. The hunt for the invisible geographic point represented by the Pole was an alien concept imported by the men from the south. The Eskimos could not imagine why anyone would be interested in territory that did not offer good hunting.

In the long run, the explorers exerted less influence on the Eskimos than the Dane, Knud Rasmussen, whose chief field of interest was the Eskimo people themselves. From the time of his first visit in 1903 until his last sojourn in the Thule district at the age of 50 in 1929, Rasmussen devoted his life to studying their ways and protecting their interests—which, he believed, were best served by strengthening their links with the rest of Greenland, then a colony of Denmark. In 1910 he set up Thule's first trading-post, where the Eskimos could exchange skins and furs for rifles, ammunition and other imported goods. With the aid of a doctor from the south, he also provided a rudimentary health service, and he established the area's first school.

By the age of 25, Itukusuk Kristiansen had won a reputation as one of the best hunters in the Thule district. His last name was bestowed on him by Greenland's Danish authorities who, during the 1960s, gave all Polar Eskimos surnames for administrative convenience. But Itukusuk's hunting skills, learned from his father Qâvigarssuaq, are firmly in the Eskimo tradition.

After his death in 1933, the Danish government took up the task. In 1937, the region was formally named Thule District and incorporated into the colony of Greenland; in 1953, its inhabitants, like other Greenlanders, became Danish citizens. In 1963, the district officially became Thule Commune; and in 1980—after home rule had been granted to Greenland—its name was altered to Avanersuup Kommunia (Eskimo for the Commune in the Far North).

At the same time that Rasmussen was setting his imprint on Thule society, important changes were also taking place in the Eskimos' spiritual life. In 1909, the first Christian missionary came to the Thule region; he was a West Greenlander by the name of the Reverend Gustav Olsen. Up to that time the Eskimos had no institutionalized system of religious belief, although they accepted the existence of spirits in the world around them and recognized the authority of shamans with power over some of the spirits. The shamans, however, put up little active resistance to the teachings of the newcomers. By 1934, every adult Polar Eskimo had been baptised into the Danish Lutheran Church and, in name at least, the Thule district was entirely Christian.

The Danish connection has inevitably brought changes to the Thule district. It has provided access to medical services, to education—all the children now normally have nine years of schooling—and to imported foods, which have eliminated the danger of starvation. These benefits would have seemed impossible luxuries to the Eskimos in the days of Qâvigarssuaq's youth.

These thoughts were very much on my mind when I last returned to the village of Moriussaq. Haunted by the image of the old man and of the stories he had told me of the past, I wanted to find out what difference, if any, the changes had made to the life of the hunters of the district.

I was pleased to find that the house in which Qâvigarssuaq and Bebiane had lived still stood. Qâvigarssuaq's son, Itukusuk, was living in it, having inherited his father's home. When I had first met him, he was a young man, living very much in the shadow of the great man's towering reputation. But with Qâvigarssuaq gone, Itukusuk cast a large shadow of his own. In his mid-thirties at the time of my last visit, he struck me as tall for an Eskimo, and he was also broad-shouldered. When he smiled, which he did frequently, he revealed a gap where his front teeth had been knocked out in a hunting accident some years before. He and his wife Sofie and their 11-year-old son Hans were still leading the roaming life of a hunting family: leaving Moriussaq as the weather and the season dictated to be near game, and returning to their home base between sorties. Itukusuk's respected status in the community was reflected in his carefully maintained hunting equipment and his large and well-fed dog team. Indeed, some of his neighbours told me that as a hunter he was even greater than his father.

Some weeks later, I was able to form a first-hand impression of his abilities when I accompanied him on a three-day trip in search of seal and arctic hare from a hunting camp on the shores of Wolstenholme Fiord. It was April, but conditions were still wintry, with temperatures well below freezing and a cutting wind. Having no sledge of my own, I planned to travel with Itukusuk.

He kept the sledge-load to a minimum. We carried a tiny, lightweight tent for overnight shelter, and a box with our cooking equipment and provisions: a battered primus stove, a plastic, two-gallon can of kerosene, a couple of cloth bags containing sugar, tea and biscuits, and a pot for brewing the tea. In addition, the sledge carried an odd assortment of smaller items that Itukusuk considered essential: bits of wire, string, spare parts for the stove, and such like. On the deck of the sledge were our harpoons, an ice-pick and a saw for cutting blocks of ice, all covered by a tough sheet of plastic. On top of that were two caribou skins, used as blankets, and our sleeping bags. The latter provided a tolerably comfortable surface on which to sit and place our rifles and Itukusuk's whip. Before we set off, Itukusuk slung over the uprights at the back of the sledge a bag containing some harpoon lines, a spare harpoon head, some spare sealskin line that could be used to mend the whip if it was broken or chewed by the dogs, a couple of pairs of sealskin mittens and a few boxes of ammunition. Hauling this comparatively light load were 14 powerful dogs—and it was no surprise to me that we covered the first 10 miles of our journey out over the sea-ice in less than an hour and a half.

In all we travelled maybe twice that distance before we found our first breathing-hole. Seals hollow networks of these tiny apertures out of the ice, to give themselves access to fresh air; for they must surface to breathe every seven to nine minutes. The holes are difficult to spot, but the experienced hunters have an almost uncanny gift for detecting them. We were moving over rough ice thinly covered with snow, without a single crack to be seen. Suddenly Itukusuk leaped off the sledge and drove the dogs off to one side.

In the twilight of a short February day, a hunter waits at a breathing-hole to harpoon a seal. Each seal has a network of holes, made by butting its nose against newly forming ice and kept open by constant use as the ice thickens. Hunters can locate the holes by the surrounding rime (right, below) formed by the frozen moisture of the seal's breath. In addition to harpoons, rifles are now often used to kill the seals as they surface for air.

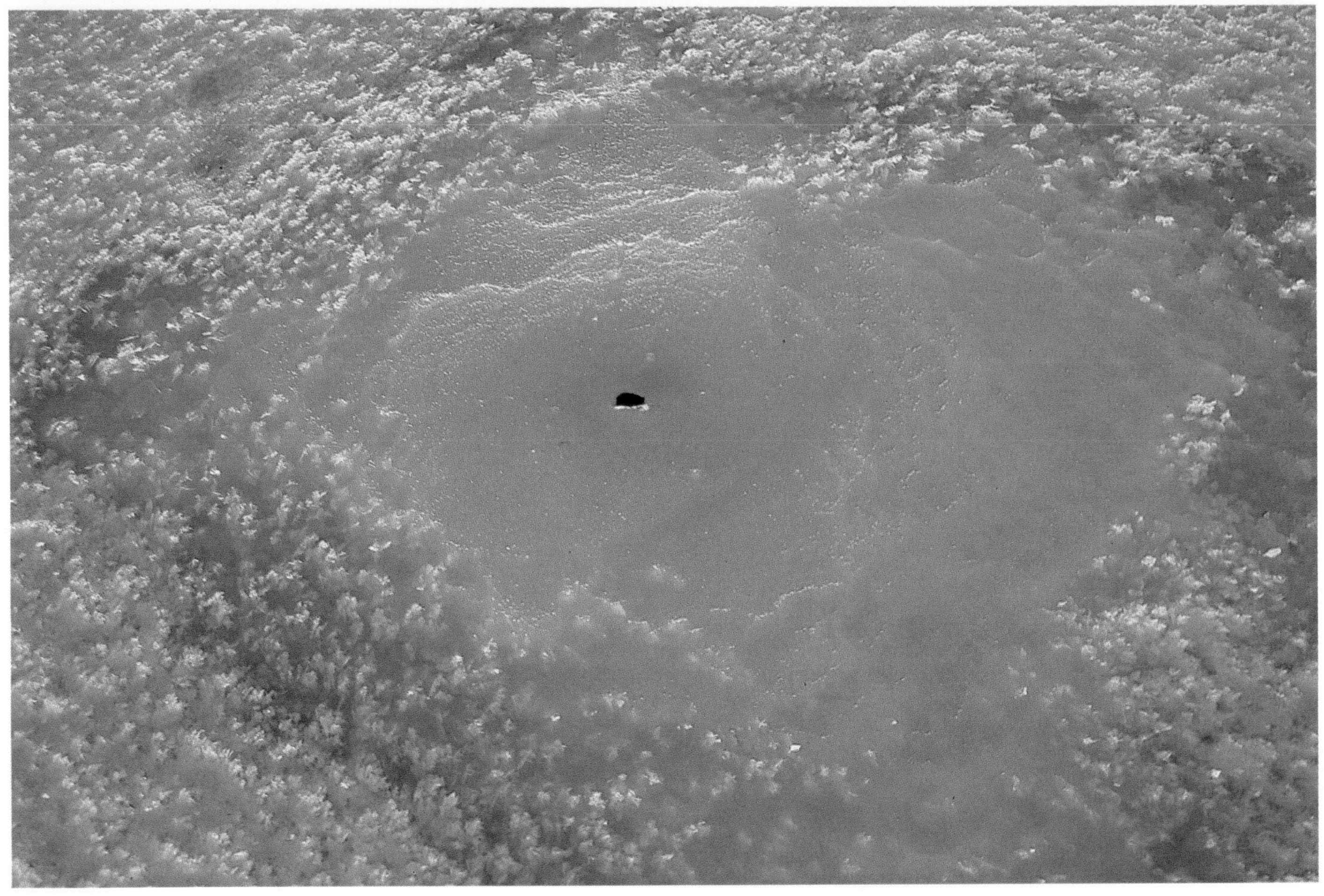

Then he sank to his knees and sniffed at the ground. Only then could I make out the hint of a mound of rime rising perhaps an inch above the snow. Using the butt-end of his whip, he made a hole in the mound. "It is fresh," Itukusuk said, scenting seal. I too got down over the hole; but I could smell only the sea.

Itukusuk returned to the sledge and handed me my rifle. For the next 30 minutes, he drove the dogs in circles about two hundred yards wide around me, hoping to drive any seals in the water in that area to the hole at which I was waiting. But no seal came and, after a time, Itukusuk lost patience and decided to move on. We found two more breathing-holes in the next four hours. At each one I stood with my rifle for half an hour or more, motionless and frozen to the core. But nothing happened."It is because the seals can smell a foreigner!" Itukusuk said, grinning broadly.

When, shortly afterwards, we found a fourth breathing-hole, I sensed that Itukusuk seemed more excited—a suspicion my companion immediately confirmed when he offered to stand watch over the hole while I drove his team around it. I had gone no farther than a hundred yards when I heard a shot. Itukusuk had killed a seal. I leaped on to the sledge as the dogs turned and raced for their master. By the time we arrived, Itukusuk had plunged a harpoon deep into the carcass to prevent it from sinking under the ice, and we quickly attached the line to the sledge. For the next 30 minutes, Itukusuk worked at the hole with his ice-pick, until it was wide enough for the dogs to haul out the seal. It was a big seal and Itukusuk was well pleased.

We had less luck the following day when, after a night spent out in the tent, we returned to the mainland coast in search of arctic hare. We climbed a steep, narrow valley that snaked up from the frozen sea to a col about 600 feet above sea level. There we again pitched our tent, in preparation for the evening, before setting off on foot, heading in different directions to increase our chances of success. Itukusuk had told me that, at this time of year, the hares were mating and that, if you stood very still, you could feel the ground shaking, so numerous were the mating pairs and so violent their passion. But although the sounds rang out all round the valley and there were tracks of hares by the hundred on every patch of snow on those slopes, neither of us saw a single animal. In spite of our lack of success, the evening back at camp was a pleasant one, as Itukusuk and I exchanged our hunting stories over a dinner of seal meat boiled over the primus stove.

The steep run down the valley the following morning was quite the most thrilling and dangerous descent with a team of dogs that I have ever made in my life. The dogs went at full tilt the whole way down, in terror that the speeding sledge would catch up with them and injure them with its metal runners. The narrow, winding valley, with its frozen stream, was strewn with huge boulders that had thundered down from the cliffs high above. With no brakes to slow our pace, the only way to ride that course without over-running and maiming several dogs was to aim the sledge so that it struck a glancing blow at each boulder that lay in our path, and to tilt the sledge up any intervening snow banks. It was a spark-flying, hair-raising plunge to sea level. Of the 19,000 miles I have so far sledged in the polar regions, those four miles were the craziest, most reckless and—I am bound to admit—the most exhilarating. Even Itukusuk, who had obviously made that descent many times, was screaming with delight.

When we reached the sea-ice and the dogs had collapsed in panting heaps, Itukusuk sank on to the snow and lay there on his back. He was heaving with laughter that seemed to rise through his body and explode from his mouth, revealing the gap where his front teeth had been. I was soon as helplessly convulsed as he was for it was impossible not to be affected by the sheer joy of life that Itukusuk spread around him. I remembered his father laughing like that years before, with an outburst of glee that could transform every human emotion and turn every serious thought upside down.

Later, when I looked back on that ride in tranquillity, Itukusuk's laughter took on a symbolic significance for me. In all its self-confident exultation, it was exactly the type of reassurance I had been seeking. I had returned to the district in search of answers to my doubts about the hunters' future, and in hope of finding some further clues that would throw light on the secrets of their survival. I had returned to talk with the Polar Eskimos, who have taught me so much. I wanted to meet again with those people to whom I—whose achievements have depended so much on my role as their unlikely protégé—owe a debt greater than I can possibly repay. I had returned to visit the graves of friends and to pay my respects to the memories of the great as well as the hard times we had shared. And in that one laugh I had found simple, unalloyed joy again—and the answers to all my questions.

A Changing Seascape

Living with their backs to the Greenland ice-sheet—a polar desert that is virtually devoid of life—the Eskimos of the Thule district look to the sea for their livelihood. For nine months of each year, from October to June, the fiords and inshore waters of the coast are frozen over, providing highways between settlements. The sea beyond is covered for hundreds of miles with a shifting surface of closely packed ice, opening up a vast hunting ground where the Eskimos pursue seal, walrus and polar bear.

Travelling by dog sledge, some hunters cover 5,000 miles a year on this icy mantle. Often they journey alone, sometimes days from the nearest

In late February, a lone hunter searches for seal where the ice meets water 10 miles out from the coast. The mist is caused by warm air from the sea

habitation. On such journeys, the hunter depends for his life on his ability to interpret the condition of the ice. Even in mid-winter, when the frozen surface may be as much as 12 feet thick, marine currents and high winds can cause the ice to break up into floes separated by channels of open water. Although the sea quickly refreezes in temperatures that plunge to –40°F, the new ice is elastic, forcing the traveller to proceed cautiously lest he set up pressure waves that can cause the icy skin first to undulate and then to crack. With the coming of spring, the ice gradually breaks up; but not until July is the sea open enough for the Eskimos to take to their kayaks.

condensing as it meets air cooled by the ice. Known as frost smoke, it warns the hunter to proceed cautiously; the ice at the water margin is wafer-thin.

Dwarfed by icebergs trapped in the frozen sea, a solitary Eskimo with his dog team and sledge follow a well-worn track at the end of May. Although the

ice is still safe enough for sledging at this time of year, the icebergs are already encircled by pools of melted ice, showing that the slow thaw has set in.

In June, an Eskimo steers his sledge to a safe fishing spot on firm ice. When travelling in early summer, hunters must distinguish between the dark blue

areas, indicating where the sea has broken through the ice, and the lighter puddles of melt-water covering ice that is still thick enough for them to cross.

In the lee of an iceberg, an Eskimo hunts seal from a kayak during July. Even at the height of summer, the sea is littered with pieces of ice that break off

melting icebergs. The Eskimos must thread their way through the debris with extreme caution since the jagged remnants can easily hole the fragile craft.

Two | Surviving the Long Polar Night

Every year, in late October, there comes a day when the Polar Eskimos see the sun slipping below the horizon and know they will not look on its light again for another four months. During the long polar night, their world becomes progressively colder, with temperatures falling to an average of −22°F in January and February. At the same time, the land is cloaked in extraordinary variations of light and dark, ranging from periods of unrelieved blackness to spells of crystal-clear twilight or moonlight so brilliantly reflected by the silvery ice-scape that the brightness dazzles the eye.

Five times I have lived with the Polar Eskimos during the transition from autumnal gloom to winter night, and I have noticed that the most magical moment comes not with the final disappearance of the sun—an event that attracts little attention—but three or four days later. It is the day, usually occurring in the last week of October, when the Eskimos awaken to find that the sea around their village has miraculously been stilled under a skin of ice.

Of all the events in the arctic year, there are few that give the Eskimos greater joy than the coming of sea-ice. They are automatically alerted to the change by the unfamiliar silence of a sea whose ragings have tormented them for weeks past. Immediately, in every shoreline settlement, people of all ages hurry down to test the new surface by prodding it with harpoons and ice-picks, then gingerly sliding out a few yards from shore. If they are satisfied that the ice will support their weight, their intent expressions give way to broad smiles; and, all at once, young and old are children together, laughing and breaking into a gentle jig to celebrate the annual surrender of the sea.

The frozen sea fundamentally changes the physical environment and heralds a more rewarding way of life. From now on, despite the darkness, the Eskimos are no longer confined to their relatively small strip of habitable land. Day by day, the area they can cover on sledges grows. By February, the sea-ice will have expanded their hunting territory more than sevenfold.

In the light of their newly won freedom, it is no wonder that the Eskimos are suddenly so elated. Over the years, however, I have come to realize that

their euphoria is an expression of relief as much as of joy, and that their emotion can be fully appreciated only within the context of the previous weeks. The freezing of the sea marks the end of one of the worst periods in the year: four or five weeks of intermittent high winds and tempestuous seas, when the salt-spray beats up from the rocks below each village and rains down on the Eskimos' houses and on their huskies lying outside. Meanwhile, within their homes, families invariably become beset by depression.

Whenever I have lived with Polar Eskimos in the autumn, I have observed the same darkness of mood building up from late September onwards. At this time, the days become shorter and storms bring to an end the brief season of hunting in boats. Increasingly, people have the feeling of being trapped within the four walls of their homes.

The quality of their housing, it is true, has been greatly improved since my first visit to the Thule district. The majority of families now live in solid, two-room wooden houses built by the workmen of the Greenland Technical Organization, or by the Eskimos themselves using prefabricated sections provided by the administration. This improved housing, together with the establishment of a general store in each village, has induced families to spend the greater part of every year based in permanent communities, instead of moving ceaselessly from one temporary settlement to another, depending on the season and local hunting conditions.

But even the newer homes are still essentially traditional inside: undecorated and sparsely furnished with a few upright wooden chairs, benches and plain tables. Moreover, being without running water, most of the houses still do not have toilets. An Eskimo simply uses the great outdoors, or—if storms are raging—a bucket placed in a corner of one room. Following centuries-old custom, the focal point of the house is the communal sleeping platform: a wooden bunk, about eight feet long and five feet wide, on which the whole family sleeps huddled together—a practice originally developed as a means of conserving body heat. At other times, the sleeping platform serves as a couch, and the large space beneath it is used for storing wooden or cardboard boxes stuffed with clothes and miscellaneous possessions.

Perhaps four or five people will live in each house: a hunter, his wife and two or three children. If the family is young, they may, for reasons of economy, be lodging temporarily in the house of the husband's or wife's parents, in which case the two couples will normally occupy separate rooms; otherwise, the second room of each house will serve as a workplace for carrying out minor repairs. In time, the young couple will get a place of their own, but they will continue to visit their elderly kinfolk often, and will bring gifts of food and skins to help supplement the pensions that all people over the age of 60 now receive from the government.

Some elderly Polar Eskimos now move to the district's main town, Qânâq, when their hunting days are over, to have access to its comforts; there is even a small communal house there for aged people of either sex who cannot afford their own home or who need special care. But most prefer to remain where they have always lived, sitting out even the uncomfortable days of autumn close to the hunting-grounds they have known from childhood.

Undoubtedly, it is the children who are least likely to suffer from the autumnal depression. Teenagers are back at the boarding-school in Qânâq by this time; and for a few hours each day, from Monday to Saturday, children between the ages of seven and 12 attend classes at their village primary school, where they are taught to read and write and to master the basic principles of arithmetic. If the bad weather keeps them indoors, the children spend their out-of-school hours listening to the adults or amusing themselves with a wide variety of indoor activities, including card games, arm-wrestling—a favourite pastime for male Eskimos of all ages—and a version of cat's cradle that involves making complicated figures with a long loop of string.

But even the children cannot remain unaware of the gloom that besets their parents at this time of year. By early October, a brooding melancholy takes root in every home. The hunters are grim-faced and silent. The women, too, are tight-lipped, bottling up their despair. However, when the hunter is away, I have seen wives break down openly and sob out their misery while their children looked on puzzled and deeply distressed because they could not console a mother whose unhappiness they did not comprehend.

It might seem ironic that the Eskimos should emerge from this darkness of the soul just as the darkness of the long polar night is closing in; but then the hunters see the loss of the sun as a challenge rather than as a threat. Moreover, there is a brief period immediately following the initial freezing of the inshore ice when they can enjoy supremely favourable conditions for hunting seal at their breathing-holes. Seal are the Polar Eskimos' most important quarry because they can be hunted all year round and because they make the greatest overall contribution to their survival. Only two species are found in the Thule region's waters throughout the year. The larger of the two is the bearded seal, weighing up to 900 pounds, which furnishes plenty of meat and a tough skin that provides the Eskimos with a hard-wearing material used for

On a windy day in late autumn, huskies scavenge for food around a family's outdoor larder: a scaffold laden with frozen seal and walrus meat. Behind the scaffold hangs the frame of a kayak, which will be built by the time the sea-ice breaks up in July.

Working by the light of a paraffin lamp and a candle in his Moriussaq home, the hunter Itukusuk fills slack winter hours replacing damaged sections of his dog sledge. In use for nine months in every year, sledges need constant maintenance as a result of the pounding they take from the bumpy terrain.

making boot soles and whip lashes. The ringed seal—a small species, averaging less than a third of the weight of its massive cousin—is found in much greater numbers. Ringed sealskins are supple and decorative, and can be sold for a good price at the trading posts as an export commodity.

Both types of seal are hunted throughout the year, though the methods used vary with the seasons. In the early summer, hunters camouflaged behind white linen screens shoot the seal as they bask on the ice. When the ice melts, they pursue them in boats. Winter techniques include laying nets to trap seal under the ice; but breathing-hole hunting is much more productive and is the Polar Eskimos' principal occupation in the cold months.

Conditions are never more propitious than in these early days of winter. The first layer of sea-ice—about three inches thick—is not strong enough to bear the weight of a loaded sledge but it is solid enough to support a hunter who ventures out on foot. Before the ice thickens—a period of four days at the most—one hunter may kill as many as 15 ringed seal and so reduce his concern about building up sufficient meat stocks for the coming months, when he will often be handicapped in his pursuit of game by darkness or treacherous ice. Each seal will provide no more than three meals for a family of four and one for the hunter's dogs. However, the sealskins can be sold and the proceeds used to buy meat from a hunter who has more than he needs.

The chances of reaping a big seal harvest at this time depend largely on the condition of the newly formed sea-ice. Ideally, the ice should be barely thick enough to bear the weight of a man, for it is when the ice is thinnest that the seal are busiest, butting out their breathing-holes that they will keep open throughout the winter by constant use. The ice must also be smooth as glass since even a thin covering of hoar-frost or snow will crunch beneath the hunter's feet, creating enough sound to scare away any quarry nearby.

This form of seal-hunting is carried out with an intentness that I can only describe as totally absorbing. Many hunters at this time use harpoons rather than rifles to kill the seal because the sound of gunshot might frighten off others. They have only a fraction of a second in which to plunge the harpoon into the skull of their prey before it submerges to safety. Every movement must be swift and silent, every wait completely motionless, and there is not a minute to lose between securing a kill and moving to a new breathing-hole; the fading noon glow that persists for two to three weeks after the sun's disappearance allows only an hour or two of hunting each day, and all the while the ice conditions are deteriorating. Within two to four days, the brief period of seal-hunting on foot is usually brought to an end because the ice becomes covered with rime as variations in the temperature—which even at this time of year may occasionally rise briefly above freezing-point—repeatedly cause the surface ice to thaw and refreeze in crystals. When this happens, even the most light-footed of hunters cannot slide on it without frightening away every seal within a half-mile radius.

It is during the first few weeks of the long polar night that one sees most strikingly how the basic pattern of life in the Thule district has remained unchanged for centuries. In their pursuit of seal over the thin sea-ice, the hunters employ methods developed by their most distant ancestors. In turn, their brief hunt provides a mountain of work for their wives, who use age-old techniques to scrape and clean sealskins, and then cut up the hides to make jackets, mittens and boots.

Although the Eskimos now buy imported shirts, jeans and undergarments at the trading stores, they still make almost all their own outer clothing which, for their purposes, is superior to even the most expensive foreign products. Inevitably, however, their outer clothing receives such hard wear that it needs constant repairing. Boot soles in particular are soon lacerated by sharp fragments of ice and need to be replaced every three or four months.

Making and mending clothes is, therefore, a never-ending chore for the hunter's wife; and it dominates her daily life in the first quarter of the long polar night. November is her busiest month, partly because she has a fresh supply of sealskins, but also because she must look ahead to Christmas, when it is customary for everyone to receive a present of clothing: usually a pair of boots, or a parka made of fox fur or caribou skin.

Meanwhile, having completed his seal-hunting over the thin ice, every hunter looks forward to realizing the dream that all polar hunters have cherished through the ages: the urge to harness up their dogs and enjoy the exhilarating sense of freedom that comes with sledging on their own far out across the new sea-ice in quest of seal or walrus. To this end, the hunters in every village work for hours, overhauling their old sledges and, if necessary, making new ones. It is all done with such urgency that one might imagine the sea-ice was going to last only a week rather than eight months or more.

In fact, there is no good reason for such haste, since the sea invariably needs a few more freezing, windless days before it is covered with a thick layer of ice extending far out from the shore. Yet there is always the same stampede to get sledges on to the new ice. It is, quite simply, a race on the part of many of the hunters—not a recognized competition, but a contest nonetheless real as the men, especially the younger ones, vie for the distinction of being the first in their village to drive a sledge on to the newly frozen sea.

This is one of the rare occasions when one is likely to see a Polar Eskimo taking a really stupid risk: driving on to flexible sea-ice that is barely five inches thick and that bends a foot or more beneath the 1,500-pound weight of a sledge and driver. I have not personally known anyone to lose his life in this foolhardy act, but I have seen a sledge cut clean through the bending ice while its young driver, holding on to the uprights at the back of the sledge, was dragged out of the water by his dog team. Yet the risk only spurs the younger men on. Like their peers all over the world, they are impatient to show their mettle and attract attention. And nothing draws greater notice than the first sledge skidding on to the new ice. It makes a glorious sight, one that stirs in the mind of every hunter his own desire to be on the move.

There is, in addition, the satisfaction of seeing a pack of powerful huskies put back to work after three months of total idleness. A team will usually consist of anything from eight to 15 dogs, though in exceptional circumstances as many as 20 dogs may be harnessed up together. At first, they are over-eager and unruly, but day by day they become more obedient until, after about 200 miles of travel, they settle down as a manageable team. At this stage, the hunter has at his command a method of polar travel that has not been improved upon in 4,000 years.

The relationship between the Eskimos and their dogs is based upon mutual respect; man and beast are equally dependent on one another to obtain the meat necessary for survival. It is also a relationship based on discipline. It is imposed within the pack by a strong king-dog and descends, by way of a pecking order, through the team; and it is imposed on the pack by the hunter, who can command his dogs to an extent that has to be seen to be believed.

With whip-cracks as loud as rifle shots, plus special calls and whistles, a skilled hunter can weave a team of dogs at full speed across the roughest stretch of ice, slow them down, stop them and get them to lie flat. He can make a 17-strong pack divide during a dangerous descent so that his sledge overruns the dogs' long traces and the team ends up behind the sledge to serve as 17 clawing anchors in the polished snow. He can drive his dogs through melt-rivers, over rocks, and up slopes with 60° gradients. He can spread them out when they are on bending ice and thereby distribute their weight for safety; and at any time he can unhitch them and make them follow him as meekly as a pack of well-trained pets.

But the husky, of course, is not a domestic animal. It is a wild dog, descended through cross-breeding from wolves, and its strongest instinct is

Wardrobes for Warmth

Although the Polar Eskimos now often wear imported clothing, their traditional attire, made from the skins and furs of the animals they hunt, is still unbeatably effective in combating the sub-zero temperatures of northern Greenland. Pelts have an important advantage over most manufactured garments: besides trapping warm air to insulate the body, they are sufficiently porous to allow the air to circulate, discouraging body moisture to keep the wearer dry and comfortable.

The heavy, thickly furred skin of the polar bear is used to make the knee-length trousers that are the pride of any hunter's wardrobe. Lighter materials such as fox fur, which provide greater freedom of movement, are preferred, however, for the parkas that keep the upper parts of the body warm in cold weather. The foxes' bushy tails are used to trim enveloping hoods, now often worn over woollen hats that provide extra protection for the head.

Because women spend less time outdoors than the menfolk, they often wear jackets that are made of sealskin, the least cumbersome, but also the least warm, of all the pelts. Stitched on to some of the jackets are hood-like pouches that provide comfortable berths for babies.

Because of its suppleness, sealskin is also the favoured material for mittens, which are provided with hanging straps so that they can be tied together when not in use, and for the knee-length boots that are everyday wear for both men and women. When travelling, or for special occasions such as weddings, some of the women wear hip-length boots made from sealskins that have been bleached in the sun to an attractive whiteness. The boots are trimmed with fringes of long polar bear hairs that bounce seductively as the wearer walks—a feature designed to add to a woman's sex appeal.

the instinct of the pack. Averaging 60 pounds in weight when fully grown, the animals possess phenomenal strength and stamina, and enough savagery to make them a danger to any stranger who ventures into their midst without a whip to establish his authority.

At the same time, a hunter can develop a strong attachment to his working dogs, especially an outstanding lead-dog that has served him faithfully for many years. I remember particularly the enormous pride that my old friend Taitsianguaratsiaq took in his dogs—without question, the strongest and biggest huskies in the Thule district. For years, when the hunter was in his seventies, his wife tried in vain to persuade him to hand over his team to his grandson and accept the dignity of old age. He steadfastly refused, taking the view that if he was too old to drive his dogs he was as good as dead.

The most nostalgic moment for hunters restricted by old age is when they see the first sledges taking to the new sea-ice early in the polar night. All at once they are reminded of the great journeys of yesteryear, of the many adventures and dangers they have undergone and will never know again. However, there is during the winter one form of hunting—requiring neither strength nor speed—that can still be practised by the veteran. This is seal-netting, an activity in which he is likely to have an advantage over younger hunters by virtue of his long experience. The art lies in deciding where to lay nets below the sea-ice while it is still relatively thin. The best spot will be at a distance from the village, where daily sledge traffic is likely to frighten away the seal. Most importantly, it will be near an iceberg that is either grounded or trapped in the ice; at these spots, air-seeking seal are attracted by cracks in the ice created by the rising and sinking of the iceberg on the tide. However, the experienced hunter will avoid an area where there are too many cracks, since this situation provides too many alternative places where the seal might come up to breathe. Ideally, the hunter finds a berg that has only one or two radial fractures around it.

To lay his nets, the hunter must first chip three holes in the ice—about 12 feet apart—all in line and each about one foot in diameter. Then he seeks to thread together the three holes by plunging into the first hole a harpoon with a nylon line attached. The idea is to angle the thrust so that the harpoon will bob up beneath the middle hole. Once the harpoon has been retrieved, the procedure is repeated until the three holes are linked by a single line some 24 feet long stretched beneath the ice. Thereafter, it is relatively simple to draw a weighted net along the line to hang like a curtain in the path of any approaching seal. Enmeshed in the net, the seal will drown. The hunter has merely to revisit the net once a week or so. He can judge by a tug on the line whether he has been lucky; if so, he hauls the net in and collects his prey.

During our stay on Herbert Island, my wife proved to have a remarkable natural talent for threading ice-holes. Time and time again, she plunged her naked arm into the freezing water and fished out her harpoon at the first attempt. Some hunters launched a harpoon many times before they managed to make it surface beneath the next hole; and afterwards, when we all retired to enjoy a brew of tea in a tent that had been set up over a sledge, there was

Games with String

During the enforced idleness of the long winter months, when bad weather and continual darkness may confine the Polar Eskimos to their homes for weeks at a time, women and children pass many hours playing games. String puzzles—a pastime similar to the Western game of cat's cradle—are particularly popular. The player holds a joined length of string taut between his hands to form a frame, then manipulates loops with his fingers and thumbs to make patterns or figures. Skilled players will often make several different string figures in sequence to illustrate a story.

Many of the figures represent familiar Polar Eskimo scenes, such as the two conically roofed houses that are connected by a porch (bottom row, left). Animals are also favourite subjects, although the designs that represent them can be so stylized as to be almost unrecognizable. Often the species are only identified by a single, easily distinguished feature, such as the bushy tail of the arctic fox (bottom row, right), or the antlers of the caribou, represented by the backward-pointing loop near the player's thumb (top row, right). Sometimes the animals are known to the Polar Eskimos only at second hand: musk oxen, identified by hanging loops that represent heads lowered for butting (top row, left), are no longer found in the Thule district.

Children are especially fond of figures that move. The snow bunting (centre row, left), for instance, "flies" up the string at the beck of a finger. Two players can join in the game of "the mouth" (centre row, right). The first player forms the shape of a mouth: a triangular opening that can be snapped shut repeatedly with a jerk of the player's thumbs. The other player then must dart a finger in and out without getting "bitten".

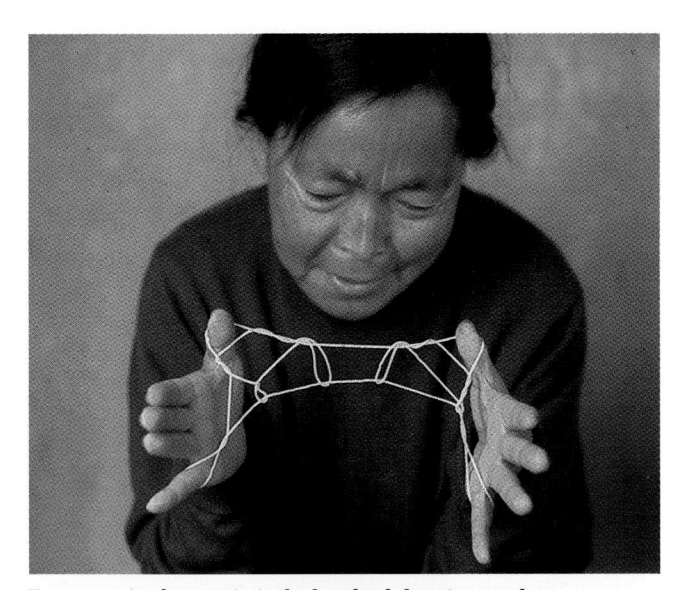

Two opposing loops mimic the heads of charging musk oxen.

The loop near the thumb represents the antlers of a caribou.

The snow bunting "flies" along the string.

The triangle snaps shut on intruding fingers.

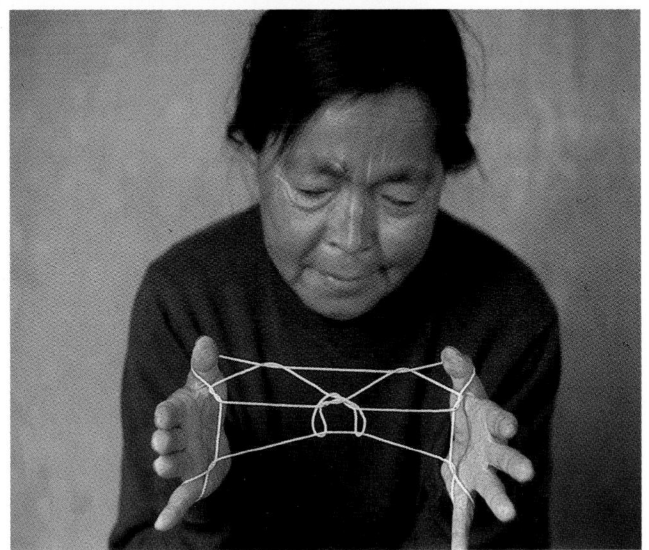

An entrance porch links two houses.

The fox is distinguished by its bushy tail.

much good-humoured teasing of those who had struggled to get their lines laid. In this respect, the work of net-laying is more fun in the company of old folk who have learnt to laugh at themselves. I have seen the job tackled almost grimly, and certainly impatiently, by eager and self-conscious young hunters who have not yet learnt that the art of living is a compromise between dignity and open-hearted fun.

The long polar night is a bewitching time of year to journey by sledge—a time that burns its brand on a traveller and makes him forever a man of the Arctic. The experience of moving across a seeming infinity of sea-ice in the winter darkness has an almost mystical quality. This is especially true when one journeys in a flood of moonlight so bright that it is possible, from a high pass or hill, to see mountains a hundred miles away. There is no setting in the world more beautiful than a polar ice-scape illuminated by a full moon high in a cloudless sky, and no Polar Eskimo child ever forgets his first awareness of this weird and unearthly light.

Often, of course, there is little or no moonlight during the four months of continuous night. But there is unforgettable excitement in travelling in pitch-darkness without stars or a compass to serve as a guide. At this time of year, I have journeyed with Polar Eskimos in the most fearful conditions imaginable. At first I was amazed by their ability to pick a tortuous route through the night. I marvelled, for example, at a hunter who could make his way in the darkness up a frozen glacial cataract to a height of 2,500 feet, cross a high pass in swirling mist and then, almost intuitively, set a course to take him through a field of crevasses to the one solitary point where the terrain allowed him to cross a moraine and enter a gully that, by way of innumerable twists and turns, led steeply down to a frozen fiord a thousand feet below.

Eventually, by harsh experience, I came to understand how this was possible. In the blackest night, the skilled hunter derives useful information from many seemingly trivial things: the way the snow lies, the direction of the wind, the angle his sledge is tilting. Every detail of the landscape is registered on his memory. His secret is having intimate knowledge of his polar world, respecting its warning signs and knowing his own limitations.

Curiously, in the early weeks of the polar night, the majority of hunters prefer to venture out on their own, responding to a compelling urge to melt into the gathering darkness, to experience the sensations of being absolutely alone and having a sense of oneness with their polar world. I myself have felt this inexplicable urge to drive out in search of a special solitude; and sometimes, when the night was blacker than the tomb, I have chanced across another lone traveller: a hunter perhaps, located only by the brief firing of a match to light a cigarette. On these rare occasions, I would immediately call my dogs to a halt and, with a flick of the whip, lay them flat on the ice. Then, on foot, I would approach the cigarette's glow, taking care to call out from afar the traditional greeting, "Inuhuarunai", meaning "Is it a human being?"

Of course, a cigarette's glow guaranteed me an affirmative reply. But there was not always a reassuring light. Sometimes, when my dogs were excited

Caught fast in the frozen sea, a column of ice—the remains of an iceberg—glitters in the winter moonlight. During the four months when the sun never appears above the horizon, the moon and stars bathe the landscape in an eerie twilight.

and refused to settle, I had only a vague sensation of another presence somewhere ahead in the darkness. Then, on approaching and asking the same question, it was always a relief to hear someone answer, "I am a human being," and so confirm that one had not, after all, walked into the arms of a polar bear. In these circumstances, a Polar Eskimo will never identify himself by name. Ask, "Who is it?" and he will say at the very most, "It is I" or "The son of a hunter", for most Eskimos have a secret dread of uttering their own name in the blackness of the night and in the company of a figure who, at a distance, remains a mystery. Although the Polar Eskimos have been Christians for over half a century, fragments of their old animist beliefs—which hold that people's names had souls of their own—linger on.

Once the first, brief heyday on the thin ice is over, seal-hunting in the polar darkness becomes an unattractive activity because the rewards are so modest in relation to the discomfort suffered. The solitary hunter may have to stand stooped over a breathing-hole for an hour or more, all the while growing stiffer and colder. Furthermore, in seeking out the elusive seal at this time of year, the hunter must rely to an unusual degree on the co-operation of his dogs who, if not well trained, may be as much a hindrance as a help.

In the darkness of the polar night it is usually impossible to detect breathing-holes by sight. Instead, the huskies must sniff them out, picking up the lingering, fishy smell that indicates the presence of a seal within the last few hours. Usually the lead-dogs are both quick and efficient in detecting recently used holes. The trouble occurs when the hunter wants to send his team away so that he can wait in complete silence for a seal to appear. Perhaps one hunter in 10 will have a supremely well-disciplined pack that, on his cry of "Huk! Huk!", will haul the sledge about a hundred yards away and then lie down to await their master's next command. Other dogs, however, will retreat too far or not far enough before lying down; and—most embarrassing of all for a hunter—a pack will sometimes cover the required distance and then keep on going, forcing their master to abandon the hole and chase after them, all the while crying out into the night for them to stop. I have heard of a team that continued all the way back to its own village 12 miles or more away, leaving their disconsolate master to trudge home after them.

Still wearing its luxuriant winter coat, an arctic fox pauses during an April forage for scraps near an Eskimo settlement. Hunters trap the foxes for their fur. Some pelts are used to make parkas and the women's traditional short pants; the rest are sold for cash at the local trading stores.

Sometimes a hunter's wife will accompany him on a seal-hunting expedition; but more often, by late November, the women are growing tired of their domestic routine and are eager for a chance to visit friends and relations in other villages. As a result, whenever the light of a full moon permits long journeys, one sees scores of families on the move. Every sledge is loaded high, and every dog capable of completing the course is harnessed in the team. In the brilliant moonlight, it makes a wonderful sight, especially when sledges from different villages happen to meet. In that situation, they will almost invariably stop to brew up some tea. I have seen 10 or more people disentangle themselves from one enormous pile of fur to join other families.

At no time in the arctic year will you see Polar Eskimo women looking happier than when, dressed in the full finery of their furs, they are involved in one of these long, moonlit social outings. Unfortunately, it is not every year that a full moon occurs at a convenient time for travelling before mid-December, when families begin to prepare for the Christmas festivities in their village and welcome the older children back from boarding school. In the event, the women must resign themselves to staying at home while every self-respecting hunter disappears for days at a time, ostensibly venturing out to search for seal or walrus, but more especially to satisfy his own pride as a man able to face the great hazards of travelling far in the polar darkness.

In dark December, the hunters who travel only as far as the seal-nets they laid in November are treated with a certain disdain by the men who roam far and wide and return with frost scars on their cheeks. A man who remains in his village may feel uncomfortable if he does not have some plausible excuse, such as illness or old age. For in this society, the hunter is supreme; and the greater his exploits in the dark, the greater the respect he commands.

It is the way of every great hunter to pretend modestly that his prestige is entirely unjustified. In contrast, his wife is likely to be much less self-effacing. She will constantly complain that she is overworked, with countless sealskins to scrape and cure. But this is really an indirect statement of pride in her husband's prowess as a hunter—a compliment which, in the company of guests, he will invariably dismiss as mere laziness on her part. No one is fooled. In every village, hunters great and small are instantly identifiable: by the number and condition of dogs they support, by the comforts they can afford to buy, by the amount of meat they can offer visitors.

Quite simply, there is an order of merit among hunters as clearly defined as the pecking order established in every pack of huskies. And yet at the same time there is an absence of social divisions in the villages of the Polar Eskimos. Everyone mixes with everyone else; every family is received with equal hospitality when visiting another family's home. And this applies no less in the case of families who may be staying only briefly in a village. However temporary their stay, they recognize that they owe allegiance to the village and automatically become an integral part of the community.

The strong community spirit that prevails in all the villages is most strikingly in evidence at Christmas, when festivities are spread over three days, beginning on December 24 with a church service, followed by a children's party. The following two days are taken up almost entirely with visiting and being visited. Every home will keep a table laden with chocolate biscuits, sweets, nuts and cigarettes to be offered to callers; and in a small village like Moriussaq, every family is expected to visit every other family. On arrival, they shake hands with every person in the house, individually wishing them a Happy Christmas, and then, with almost painful self-consciousness, they distribute small gifts, each neatly wrapped in festive paper.

An air of quite uncharacteristic gentility pervades the greater part of the celebrations. Suddenly, when visiting a family, one discovers that they have saucers to accompany their cups; conversely, there is no sign within the house of the familiar tub that is usually filled with the thawing blubber and guts of some slaughtered mammal. Floors are scrubbed clean, the walls adorned with religious pictures and plastic holly, the rooms are aglow with candles that have been welded by their own wax on to metal jam-jar lids, or shaved and inserted into the necks of empty liquor bottles.

The people themselves present a different image. Everyone is wearing his finest clothes—men and boys in spotless white parkas with polar bear-skin pants or black trousers; women in white blouses with embroidered collars, open-necked parkas, traditional, tight-fitting fox-skin pants and thigh-length boots of white sealskin so stiff that their wearers move with an awkward, swinging gait; little girls in party dresses or, like their mothers, in pretty parkas, fox-skin pants and long boots.

On the third evening of Christmas, each village has a community party for adults. Then the fun-loving character of the Polar Eskimos begins to show through the veneer of genteel respectability. The villagers gather in the schoolroom or in one of the larger houses. Usually, on this one occasion of the year, the men wait upon the women, serving them with coffee or tea, biscuits, bread and jam. Every party begins formally enough, but gradually the jokes exchanged become more ribald, and then the guests move on to party games that become progressively less dignified as the evening wears on.

Especially popular is a guessing game that involves passing from hand to hand, beneath a table, an object prepared by one of the party's organizers. All the players are commanded to close their eyes while the mystery object is slipped into the hands of the person at the head of the table. Each person, in turn, must then feel the object all over and try to identify it. The success of the game rests on making the "thing" as revolting as possible to the touch and seeing the reaction of everyone who holds it in his or her hands.

When I last joined in this guessing game, the first object to be passed round the players was small and roundish in shape, clammy and furry to the touch. Somehow it seemed positively obscene. In fact, it proved to be nothing more than a soft-boiled egg that had been shelled, covered with the fine-haired underbelly skin of a dead husky pup and then dampened with water. It was, nevertheless, sufficiently well disguised to produce extraordinary reactions of horror and disgust from Eskimos who were accustomed to killing, flensing, butchering and tanning animals of all shapes and sizes and who regularly came into contact with steaming blood and guts, or the cold and reeking, thawed-out carcasses of animals that had been dead for months.

Each woman shrieked when she felt the object that had been handed to her. The men imitated the screams of the women, and the laughter rose to near hysteria as the players made very basic guesses as to the nature of the object. All at once, the Eskimos were released from the constraints of a piety they had learnt from foreigners; they were themselves again, forcefully demonstrating their innate and passionate love of gaiety.

After the Christmas festivities are over, life reverts to the perpetual quest for seal and walrus out on the ice. My first experience of hunting walrus in the last few weeks of a long polar night is still a vivid memory. Towards the end

Hunting the Walrus

Walrus hunting calls for cool nerve and quick wits, but the rewards are on a grand scale. A full-grown male walrus weighs as much as one and a half tons: enough meat and blubber to feed a family of four and their dogs for two months.

Walrus live in herds up to 20 strong and have traditional territories, near rocky shores, where they feed on shellfish. They are hunted all year round, but with special dedication in winter, when other game is scarce. During this season, they stay under thin ice so that they can smash breathing-holes with their heads. Here lies the hunter's greatest danger: to get close enough to harpoon a walrus, he must deal with his prey on ice that is less than six inches thick.

Because of the risk, walrus hunters usually operate in pairs or larger groups. After travelling by sledge to an area where walrus are known to congregate, the hunters leave their sledges at the edge of the thick ice nearer shore and continue on foot, walking in single file to minimize noise and testing the ice ahead with their harpoons. Once they spot a breathing-hole, they approach cautiously, listening for the characteristic snorts a walrus makes as it surfaces.

When the walrus next comes up for air, the lead hunter throws his harpoon as hard as he can to penetrate the creature's hide. As the point hits home, he runs back to thicker ice and anchors the line. Speed is vital: immediately on being hit, the walrus dives, and seconds later it may crash up through the ice where the hunter was standing, in an attempt to gore him with its tusks.

When the walrus does reappear—whether to attack or simply to breathe—the hunter kills it with a rifle. Then men and dogs combine their strength to haul the huge carcass out of the breathing-hole and back to thick ice.

Edging warily over thin ice, a hunter prepares to harpoon a walrus as it comes up for air (right, above). As the prey starts to dive, he hurls his weapon (right), aiming for the soft underside of a front flipper. Having raced to secure the harpoon line to an ice-pick stuck into the ice behind him, he stands on the line (inset) to reduce leverage on the anchor and prevent it from tearing loose.

The harpoonist watches while his hunting partner cuts two slits in the skin of the dead walrus (left) to form a loop of thick hide through which a tow-line can be passed. The line is then hitched to the hunters' two dog teams, which combine their strength to drag the heavy walrus on to thick ice (inset, below), where it is butchered.

of January, I had set off from Herbert Island in the company of my friend Avataq, the hunter. We were journeying over the ice of Whale Sound, heading for the coast of Steensby Land, where we hoped to find walrus at their breathing-holes in the new ice. As we moved off, I looked up at the sky and saw, at long last, a pale, refracted hint of the returning sun.

In the bitter cold, with the fog of breath streaming from the dogs, we travelled for some four hours until, in the far distance, I saw two sledges—one of them covered with a makeshift tent held up by two harpoons stuck in the snow. When we drew alongside this sledge, we found that the occupants of the tent were Avataq's septuagenarian father, Taitsianguaratsiaq, and his wife, who were snuggled inside, drinking mugs of tea brewed on a primus stove. My hunting companion, who was busy untangling the traces of his dogs, told me to go in and join them. For half an hour I shared the fug of steam and warmth within the tent. Then, shortly before we moved on, I asked the old man where he was heading. He did not say. He simply chuckled and replied, "Maybe we, too, will hunt the walrus."

His wife sighed. "But the walrus will hear you breathing and go away."

"Then, woman," he growled, "I shall hold my breath."

He immediately proceeded to give us a demonstration, holding his breath until he was blue in the face and had scared us half to death. Finally, after what seemed an eternity, he gasped out air and burst into raucous laughter.

The next day, having invited the old folk to join us, we did get our walrus. Avataq led the way, while we ventured cautiously in his footsteps over the new ice that stretched for about a mile from the coast. Eventually we came to an area scarred with many holes, each two or three feet across. I wondered how such large holes had been created, and I was about to ask when my question was answered: less than 20 feet away, the enormous head and tusks of a bull walrus—representing one and a half tons of meat and blubber—smashed through the thin ice. It gazed short-sightedly in our direction for several seconds with its startled, bloodshot eyes, then sank out of sight.

I have never felt more vulnerable. Twice more the walrus surfaced, each time a little nearer to us. My companions signalled me not to move; and for three minutes—the longest three minutes of my life—I remained rooted to the spot. Then, at last, the walrus surfaced a fourth time, only 10 feet away. Avataq was ready. He rushed forward and thrust his harpoon deep into the walrus' neck. As the beast sank back into the sea, Avataq took up his ice-pick, drove it into the soft new ice, looped the harpoon line round it, and then braced his foot against the handle of the pick as the line played out.

Meanwhile, the old man was quickly chipping two small holes in the ice with his long hunting-knife just a few feet from the ice-pick handle. With an undercutting action, he then hacked a six-inch tunnel which linked the two holes together. Through this tunnel he looped the tail end of Avataq's harpoon line to secure it firmly. Hand over hand, the two hunters now hauled on the line to pull the wounded walrus back to the last hole it had made. As it reappeared, the huge creature raised its great tusked head above the ice and blew out a loud spluttering snort. While the old man strained to hold the line alone, Avataq reached for his rifle and, at point-blank range, fired a single shot. The bullet went straight through the walrus' brain.

By far the most difficult part of the hunt was hauling the dead walrus on to the sea-ice. We used two teams of dogs and a block and tackle, but when the 12-foot-long walrus was almost half way out of the water, the surrounding ice began to give way under its enormous weight. Avataq at once climbed on to the back of the walrus and opened up the carcass along its length with his knife so that, on our next attempt, its weight would be more widely distributed on the ice. His cunning did the trick: the dogs strained against the end of their traces, and all at once the carcass came free.

Because of the thin ice, it had taken us four hours to haul the walrus from the sea. Now, in the fading light, we worked for another three hours flensing the walrus and transporting the meat back to the safety of dry land, a mile away. So great was the amount of meat—more than 10 times the quantity provided by one ringed seal—that we needed to make two journeys, with each of our three sledges fully loaded. By the time we had finished, the night was black as pitch and we were utterly exhausted. But it was a joyful tiredness, and for a long time afterwards the four of us sat together in the old folk's tent, reliving the excitement of the hunt and laughing as each hunter perversely teased the other about his fear and made light of his own.

A few weeks later, in mid-February, I was still travelling with Avataq when the polar night ended. Our sledges had temporarily become separated and when I caught up with him, I witnessed something I have never seen again in all my subsequent visits to the Arctic. In the far distance, I saw him performing his own private greeting to the returning sun.

For a few minutes, Avataq stood gazing at the sun as it slowly crept above the horizon. As its light flooded across the silvery plain, he pushed back the hood of his parka and bared his head. Throwing his hands high, he turned the palms outwards so that they were bathed in the brilliant red glow.

Avataq did not know I was watching him. For a long time I did not move for fear of revealing my presence and so marring what was clearly a personal and spiritual moment. In that moving gesture, when he celebrated the end of four long months of darkness, it was as though he and the sun were one in spirit—and its warmth and light gave him fresh hope and energy, just as surely as it infused new life into the polar world.

The Indispensable Husky

Little sentiment exists in the relationship between a Polar Eskimo and his team of dogs. During the first four months of life, the puppies are carefully nurtured and even brought into the home as children's pets, but thereafter the huskies live entirely outdoors and must earn their keep hauling their master's sledge.

To train young dogs for work the Eskimos run them, in increasingly long sessions, with fully trained animals. During this period, the young dogs learn to respond to the whip and to oral commands, and they also establish a place for themselves in the pecking order of a team. Those too weak to

Lips drawn back from their powerful jaws, two full-grown huskies snarl into the icy morning air while they are waiting to receive food. Descended

stand the pace, or too unruly to fit in with the other dogs, are usually killed. At seven months, the survivors are put to harness for the rest of their days.

Huskies rarely live beyond 10 years. In their life, however, they travel a total of thousands of miles to and from far-flung hunting grounds, often hauling loads of 400 pounds or more and going two or three days at a time without food. In the harsh polar environment, their harnessed power is still the most efficient means of crossing snow and ice, and a dog team—ranging in number from five to 15, the size reflecting its owner's prosperity and skill—remains the most prized possession of every Eskimo hunter.

through cross-breeding from wolves, the dogs can sometimes show great savagery and so they are treated with caution even by their own masters.

Still harnessed to a sledge, a bitch suckles her three-week-old pups during a brief halt on a springtime hunting trip. After giving birth, a husky rests with her litter for two weeks. Then she must resume work in the dog team accompanied by her pups, which ride on the sledge, usually wrapped in a sack cut with holes for breathing.

In his father's house, a 15-month-old Eskimo boy introduces a husky pup to his toy whip. The education works two ways. The pup becomes accustomed to being handled; the young boy learns how to use a whip—an essential skill for keeping huskies under control. The dogs quickly develop obedience to the whip; its sound alone is usually enough to bring unruly dogs to order.

A hunter adjusts the harness strapped around the shoulders of one of his dogs. A harness is individually fitted to every husky and is removed only for adjustment or repairs. To discourage dogs from gnawing through the straps and breaking loose, a hunter may file down his huskies' teeth.

To protect its paws from the sharp crystals of early summer ice, a dog is fitted with boots fashioned from squares of rubberized canvas and securely bound to the legs with twine. Two small holes are cut in the bottom of each boot to allow the dog's middle claws to protrude and gain a foothold on the ice.

Harnessed in a fan formation, a team of huskies hauls a fully loaded sledge across snow-covered ice. In this formation—ideal for crossing treacherous

terrain—the lead-dogs, usually the strongest and most intelligent animals, can pick out the surest route for the less canny dogs trailing them to follow.

On an early summer fishing trip, a hunter and his lead-dog assess the problem of how the sledge and dog team are going to cross a wide channel in the sea-ice.

At a point where the channel narrows, the hunter, whip in hand, leaps across ahead of the dog team.

Summoned by their master's call and whip, some dogs fall short in the jump and land in the water.

The hunter hauls out a dog wearing boots. When reunited, the dog team will pull the sledge across.

From a safe distance, a hunter feeds his dogs by throwing to each in turn a chunk of frozen walrus meat. The food was retrieved from a stone-marked cache where it was left on an earlier expedition. Normally teams eat fresh meat, which is easier to digest. The huskies often go for three days without food, but after a big kill at the end of a long, hard haul, a dog will be fed all the meat it can eat—sometimes as much as 30 pounds.

Spread out in a star pattern on the sea-ice, a team of huskies awakens to a new day. One dog (extreme right) has chewed its way out of its harness. But the pack instinct is strong and the dog stays close to the other huskies, which remain securely tethered on their long traces, which are looped through a narrow tunnel chiselled out of the ice.

A Day in the Life of **Savfak Kivioq**

It was seven o'clock on a mid-April morning, and the sun had already been shining for five hours. Yet nothing stirred in the hunting settlement of Narssârssuk, a tattered string of wooden shacks facing the frozen waters of Wolstenholme Fiord. The only sound was the sighing of a bitterly cold south-west wind. Outside each shack, huskies lay still as corpses on the icy ground.

Within one of the shacks, Savfak Kivioq slipped out of the bed she shared with her husband and two of her children. In her late thirties, she was still a handsome woman, despite the wrinkles that an oppressive climate and onerous cares had etched upon her face. Still heavy with sleep, she dressed quickly, pulling a thick woollen sweater and cotton slacks over the woollen vest, tights and socks she had been wearing in bed. Then, shivering in the chilly room, she lit a primus stove and put on a pan of water to make herself a cup of instant coffee. The hut was heated by an old cast-iron coal stove, but supplies of the fuel were running short and so the stove had been allowed to burn low overnight; it gave off barely enough heat to keep out the cold—at −16°F, the temperature was below average for the time of year.

The rest of the family remained in bed, snug beneath their quilts. The bed, in typical Polar Eskimo style, was a mattress-covered wooden platform that extended the width of the shack. Savfak's husband Asiajuk, a 41-year-old hunter, lay beside his young son Qajoránguaq. His daughter Aininaq—who was aged 11, one year older than Qajoránguaq—was curled up at her brother's feet.

The Kivioqs had been married for 20 years. In all they had six children; but the four eldest, all daughters, were away at the boarding school in Qânâq attended by every Polar Eskimo teenager. Both Savfak and Asiajuk came from hunting families, so even before their marriage they were well accustomed to the nomadic lifestyle that the never-ending search for fresh game entails. They rarely spent more than six months of the year in their own home—a larger shack in the village of Moriussaq 25 miles away. The rest of their time was divided between temporary hunting camps and borrowed huts such as the one in which they were currently living. It belonged to a hunter friend who was spending the first few months of the year at his home in Qânâq. Such loan arrangements are fairly common between the Polar Eskimos, who are constantly on the move.

That morning, as every morning, Savfak's first job was to prepare the family's sealskin boots. Each boot consists of three parts: a knee-length outer casing of sealskin and, fitted within it, a pad of wadding and a long sock usually made of sheepskin from south-west Greenland or the supple skin of the arctic hare. Worn by all Polar Eskimos throughout the year, the boots are supremely effective in keeping out the cold, but they do not provide complete protection against damp. Wet

Husband Asiajuk lingers in bed.

sealskin stiffens as it dries overnight, so the boots have to be softened each morning to restore their flexibility.

To accomplish this task, Savfak sat on the edge of the bed, using her feet and her knees to hold a long stick, shaped like an inverted "T", with a semi-circular metal head. Pulling one of Asiajuk's boots on to the stick, she rubbed the inner sole over the iron head until the skin was soft and flexible. Next, Savfak took a long strip of cotton-wool and folded it over twice to make a wad of three layers. She fitted the pad into the sole of the boot to provide extra insulation against the cold and to absorb humidity and sweat. Finally, she pulled a sheepskin sock over the boot-stretcher and tugged the softened boot over the sock so that they fitted smoothly together, with the cotton-wool padding sandwiched between.

After Savfak had prepared his pair of boots, Asiajuk summoned the energy to get dressed and make himself some coffee. Puffing at his pipe, he gazed listlessly through the clear plastic sheeting used in the shack's windows as a cheap substitute for glass. The day was raw and chilly, and he had little enthusiasm for hunting. Handicapped by poor eyesight, he had never been one of the district's most successful hunters. But he knew the family's food supplies were running low. Hunting conditions had been bad and the stock of seal meat was almost exhausted. What little remained was needed to feed the huskies, to keep them strong for hunting trips. The family were making do for the time being with hard-tack biscuits, soup, margarine and jam they obtained from the trading post at Dundas, 12 miles away.

The Kivioq family had been in Narssârssuk for four months, but they had little to show for their labours. Normally the hunting grounds near the settlement are well stocked with both seal and walrus, and even a hunter of limited ability could count on feeding his family and building up a stock of skins to sell at the trading posts. This year, however, the family had barely kept body and soul together. Asiajuk was restless; he wanted to return to Moriussaq by the beginning of May.

Their temporary home offered few inducements to prolong their visit. Like all the shacks in Narssârssuk, it was built of old pieces of timber patched up with strips

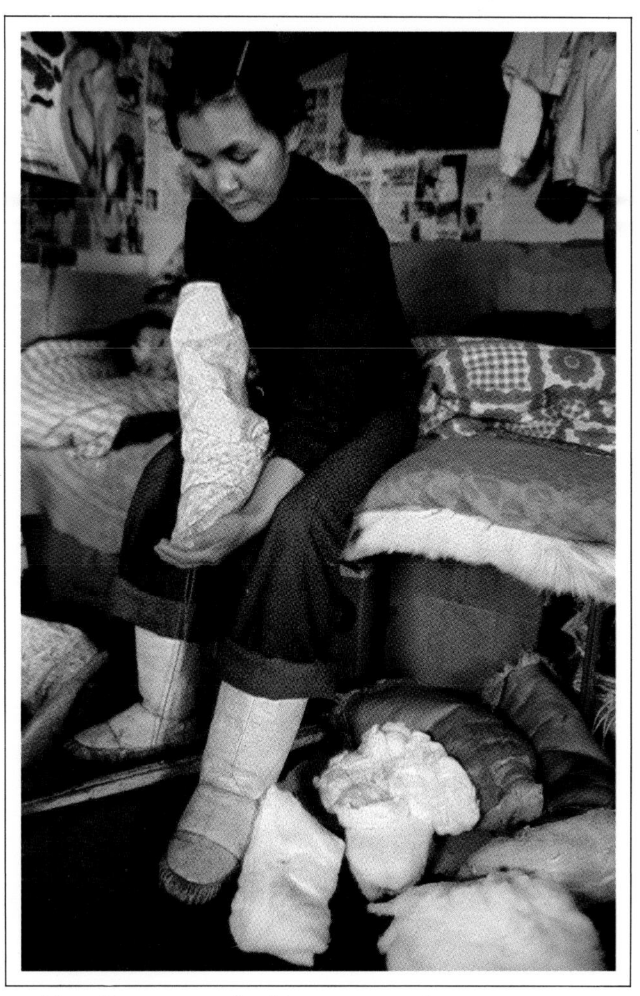
Savfak stuffs cotton-wool padding into Asiajuk's boots.

of wood from packing crates. To conserve warmth, it had a double entrance: two front doors separated by a three-foot-long passageway constructed of wood. The inner, wooden door was fixed slanting inwards to make it self-closing and the outer opening was protected by a simple canvas flap. As an extra measure to keep out draughts, the Kivioqs had covered the inside walls of the hut with an impromptu collage of pages torn from magazines. But the cold air still found its way through. In Narssârssuk, winds of as much as 100 m.p.h. are common and the settlement's makeshift houses literally had to be anchored to the ground. Strong nylon or metal ropes were strung taut across the roof of each dwelling, with their ends tightly secured to large steel drums weighted down with rocks.

After lingering for an hour or more over his pipe and coffee, Asiajuk finally announced that he was going out to hunt. On hearing this, Qajoránguaq fairly tumbled out of bed. Although he rarely got the chance to accompany his father, he loved helping him to get ready for hunting trips. His high spirits made it impossible for his sister, Aininaq, to sleep on, and so—without the same enthusiasm—she got dressed, too. Aininaq had little interest in hunting. While she stayed in Narssârssuk, her education consisted chiefly of watching her mother at work and helping round the house, learning the skills that are needed by a hunter's wife.

While Aininaq and Qajoránguaq shared a meagre breakfast of coffee and hard-tack biscuits, Savfak went out to collect some ice to provide water for washing and drinking. There is no piped supply in the Thule district, except in Qânâq; ice is the only source of water. Since sea-ice is salty, each family stores a stock of salt-free ice that is transported by sledge from the nearest iceberg—a chore that sometimes involves a two-hour journey over the frozen sea. Chunks of ice are brought indoors as they are needed. Savfak used an old pair of scissors to hack a piece from the pile outside their shack, then carried it inside and left it to thaw in a large metal tub.

It was almost 10 o'clock before Asiajuk was finally ready to go hunting. All the family went outside to help. While Savfak wielded a 25-foot-long sealskin whip to keep the dogs grouped together, her husband untangled the huskies' traces and hitched them to the sledge. The

A store of glacial ice provides water.

The ice will be melted on a stove in the borrowed wooden shack.

Flicking a whip, Savfak helps to round up the dog team before her husband sets off to hunt.

children helped their father to load the sledge with a primus stove, a can of kerosene, a tent, and a supply of biscuits, margarine, tea and sugar. Asiajuk planned to make only a short trip, but no Polar Eskimo hunter ever takes chances; he always carries a tent and some provisions with him in case the weather suddenly changes and forces him to make camp.

Last to be lashed into place on the sledge was the hunting gear: a harpoon, a rifle and an ice-pick. Then Asiajuk led the dogs cautiously over the rough ice lining the shore. Once they had reached the smoother sea-ice beyond, he jumped on the sledge and, with a cry of "Huko! Huk! Huk!" and a crack of his whip, set the dogs trotting on their way. At first the children slid along behind him, hanging on to the wooden uprights of the sledge. Then, as the dogs gradually gathered speed, they let go and ran after the sledge, waving and shouting until their father was too far off to hear.

Asiajuk was using only 11 of his 12 dogs that day. The stay-at-home was a bitch about to whelp; she remained tethered to a rock near the house. Before going back indoors, Savfak checked the lead to be sure it was securely fixed, then threw the husky a chunk of seal meat.

The children meanwhile had gone off to play with friends at one of the other houses. By law, Polar Eskimo children are supposed to start schooling at the age of seven. In practice, however, this is often impossible, since their families are frequently on the move to fresh hunting grounds. In Narssârssuk, where there was no school, Qajoránguaq and Aininaq spent most of their time playing or sleeping. Indoors, they enjoyed games like draughts or yatse, a form of poker dice popular with Polar Eskimos of all ages; outdoors, they joined up with the neighbours' children, sliding on the ice or hitching up young dogs to pull their small sledge.

A pregnant husky bitch needs special attention.

With her husband and children out of the hut, Savfak started on her main job of the day: treating the skin of a ringed seal that Asiajuk had killed a week before. Preparing sealskin is the predestined lot of Eskimo women, an endlessly repeated household chore that requires skill and, above all, patience. After a kill, the hunter must flense the animal within a few hours to prevent the skin from discolouring. Then it is stored out of doors where, in the sub-zero temperatures, it keeps in perfect condition until the hunter's wife is ready to clean it.

Before she began, Savfak used a stone to sharpen her skinning tool, a multi-purpose household knife consisting of a sharp, semi-circular blade inserted in a short wooden handle. Asiajuk had fashioned the tool from a piece of scrap wood and an old saw blade.

Sitting down on the edge of the bed, Savfak stretched a section of the sealskin over a square wooden board, the top of which she rested against her knee. She placed the foot of the board in a wooden box on the floor in front of her, then, with downward movements of the knife, began to scrape off the blubber into the box. Through years of practice she was able to work quickly without cutting the skin. As each part of the skin was cleared of fat, she folded it back under the board, thus stretching out a new section for scraping.

She scrapes blubber from a sealskin.

The range is fuelled sparingly with coal.

When the entire sealskin was scraped clean, Savfak placed it in a metal tub containing a chemical cleaning agent, where it would remain for 24 hours until the last traces of blubber had been dissolved. Meanwhile, she set to work on another sealskin that had been left to soak the day before. The first task was to rinse out the chemical, so Savfak stoked up the coal stove and melted down some ice in a large pan. After rapidly immersing the skin in the water, she hung it from a hook in the ceiling to drain briefly, then squeezed out the excess moisture. Finally, she carried the pelt outside to the back of the house and hung it out to dry on a wooden clothes-rack, which was covered with plastic to prevent the wet skin from freezing on to the wood.

Even after a day on the rack, the skin would not be completely dry. On the following day, Savfak would have to cut small holes at intervals round the edge of the skin, then thread the holes with thick nylon string and lash the skin to the sides of a wooden frame. Stretched within this frame, the skin could be left to dry out thoroughly without danger of shrinking or wrinkling.

At the Dundas trading post, the prepared skin would be graded and Asiajuk would receive a down-payment varying according to its quality. In summer, the skin would be shipped to Copenhagen and sold at auction. If it fetched a higher price than the down-payment, the hunter would receive the balance at the end of the year, less about 20 per cent for handling charges. The sale of prepared skins is usually a hunter's main source of cash, providing the wherewithal for buying food, fuel, ammunition and other supplies.

It was now early afternoon and Savfak began work on a pair of sealskin boots she was making for one of her daughters in Qânâq. A good seamstress, Savfak occupied herself making clothes throughout the year, whenever the necessary skins could be kept back for family use. In good years, when game was plentiful, she was especially busy as Christmas approached, preparing time-consuming outer garments, such as fur jackets and trousers of polar bear skin, to provide Asiajuk with the strong, watertight gear he would need for the next year's hunting. Mostly, however, she spent her time making smaller items of clothing: sealskin boots and mittens, and colourful woollen hats that Polar Eskimo women crochet in spiral fashion for their menfolk.

To make the boots, she began by cutting out the rough shapes of two soles from a piece of bearded sealskin—a tougher, less pliable material than the depilated skin of the ringed seal used for the uppers. She occasionally used a piece of string to measure lengths, but through the years she had made so many boots that she did not need to work to a pattern.

Before the soles could be sewn on to the uppers, the skin had to be softened to make it flexible. Traditionally, Eskimo women soften skins by chewing them; this method avoids damaging the fibre, which would make the skin less waterproof. However, Savfak, like many hunters' wives, had lost all her teeth through decay and

Savfak pegs the cleaned skin to dry on a plastic-covered rack.

The sole of a sealskin boot must be softened.

she had been provided with dentures by a Danish dentist who visited the settlements each year. She therefore had to soften the skin by laying it on a flat rock and pounding it with a hammer. Repeatedly she bent the sole and beat along the folded edge, thus creating a series of softened ridges. When both soles were ready, she rolled them up inside a damp cloth to keep the skin moist and make it easy to sew the following day.

In typical Eskimo fashion, Savfak worked as necessity demanded or as the mood took her, taking up work unfinished from the previous day or setting up a task to be continued later. For example, after finishing work on the boot soles, she picked up a boot that she had almost completed the day before and began to sew on the edging that houses the drawstring used to hold up the boots.

In the past, all Polar Eskimo women used sinew from the narwhal as thread because it swells when wet, ensuring a watertight seam. But Savfak, like most hunters' wives nowadays, used dental floss, a popular modern substitute because it is exceptionally strong and does not tear the skin being sewn.

Growing tired of sewing, Savfak put down the boot to take a break. It was now the middle of the afternoon. She

Carrying her own cup, Savfak sets off for coffee and a chat at a neighbour's house.

Friend Sofie (left) entertains Savfak and a young neighbour.

decided to go and see Sofie, the wife of Itukusuk the hunter who was living temporarily in a nearby shack.

In the small world of Narssârssuk, Savfak's entire social life revolved round such visits to the seven or eight other families who were living at the time in the settlement. As usual, she took one of her own coffee cups with her. Coffee or tea is invariably offered to guests by the hostess; and, as a matter of course, each visitor brings his own mug—a tradition stemming from the days when drinking vessels were in short supply.

On this occasion, Savfak arrived to find Sofie chatting with the daughter of another neighbour. The women greeted her warmly. After hostess and guest had exchanged pleasantries, Sofie gestured to a plastic-lined bowl on the floor in the centre of the room. It contained two large knives and some cold seal liver.

Eskimos do not stand on ceremony; when food is offered, visitors are free to help themselves. Savfak, who had eaten nothing all day except a few biscuits, was hungry. She squatted on the floor, picked up a large chunk of meat and, in Eskimo style, ate it by sawing off pieces as she held the meat between her teeth. Then she helped herself to coffee and joined the others on the sleeping platform—which, as is usual in one-roomed Eskimo homes, doubled as a couch during the day.

News travels quickly round the Thule district, relayed by hunters moving from one hunting ground to another. This afternoon, Sofie had a dramatic story to recount. A local hunter—one of the best in the Thule district—had just had a serious accident. His dogs had picked up the trail of an arctic fox. They had pursued their quarry on to an iceberg but in the excitement of the chase had failed to see a crevasse ahead of them, and all the dogs and the fox had plunged to their deaths, the sledge falling with them. The driver had seen the danger just in time and managed to jump to safety. With night falling, he had walked miles to reach shelter.

The women gossiped and drank coffee for two hours before Savfak decided it was time to return home. As she approached her shack, her children ran to meet her. They had spent the afternoon playing in another neighbour's home where they too had been given a meal.

By that time it was 6.30 p.m. After doing some mending, Savfak began tinkering with a primus stove that needed cleaning. The Kivioqs had four primus stoves,

She helps herself to a snack of cold seal liver.

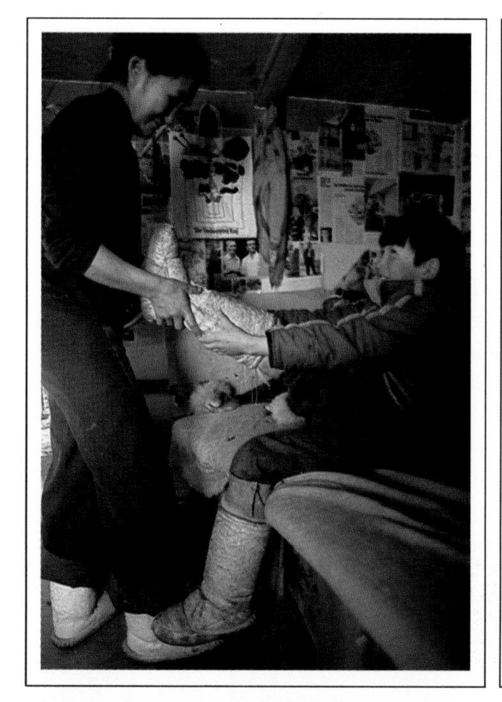

Son Qajoránguaq needs help with his boots.

Asiajuk returns home with the day's catch—a brace of ptarmigan.

but only two were in working order. One was constantly in use for both heating and cooking, and the other her husband had taken with him. As often happened, the two non-functioning stoves had become clogged by soot from the low-quality kerosene that burned in them. By pricking the jet repeatedly with a piece of thin wire, Savfak finally got one of them working again.

As she was finishing the task, the children spotted their father's sledge moving across the sea-ice towards the shack. Savfak helped the children to pull on their boots, then the family went outside, impatient to see the day's catch. But the trip had not been a success: the only game Asiajuk had on his sledge was a brace of scrawny ptarmigan, a species of grouse that is common in the Arctic all through the year.

The family hid their disappointment. The birds were too small to provide a proper meal for everyone. For the second time that day, the Kivioqs had to satisfy their hunger with some hard-tack biscuits and coffee.

After the meal, the children settled down on the sleeping platform to browse through some comic books. They giggled happily at the pictures, even though they could read barely a word of the Danish text. The parents

The birds may, or may not, be worth cooking.

spent the evening carving ivory. Both of them were adept at making small grotesque figures, half-human and half-animal, known as *tupilaks*. These gargoyle-like creatures, carved out of walrus tusks, whale teeth or stone, are then sold at the trading stores for export as ornamental curiosities.

With his real talent for working in ivory, Asiajuk always found a ready market for his pieces in Dundas. Indeed, his carvings sold so well that his income as a carver often exceeded his meagre earnings as a hunter. But he got less satisfaction from his artistry than from his hunting trips. Even a poor Polar Eskimo hunter takes pride in his way of life, and Asiajuk could not reconcile himself to being dependent on other hunters, even at a price, to provide meat for his dogs. So, rather than developing his talent, he carved only when he felt like it or when immediate needs demanded.

At midnight, shortly after sunset, the Kivioqs went to bed. It had been a disappointing day.

Their fortunes improved next day. Savfak accompanied her husband on a hunt, which she often did. She waited with a rifle at a breathing-hole while Asiajuk circled the opening on his sledge, hoping to drive seals towards her. Two seals came to the hole and Savfak shot them, solving the family's food problems—for the time being, anyway.

Carving a whale's tooth will add to the family's funds.

Three | Longer Days, Longer Journeys

From that spectacular moment in February when the sun first reappears over the ice of Baffin Bay, travelling conditions in the Thule district steadily improve. It signals the season for long sledge journeys. The hours of daylight lengthen at a rate of 20 minutes or more a day. The ice, too, continues to grow thicker and firmer since, despite the sun's reappearance, February and March are the two coldest months of the year, with temperatures frequently falling to –20°F. Not until after mid-April, when the sun once again still shines at midnight, does the melting of the snow and ice begin.

However, sledging conditions are not uniformly good at this period, any more than they are at other times of the year. True, the fast ice near the shoreline that has not been dislodged by high tides or strong winds has by now reached a thickness of between two and three feet. But where the winds blow down from the glacial valleys, continually breaking up the ice and then driving the floes out to sea, new ice forms in a thin layer that may not be firm enough to bear the weight of a sledge. When you are travelling in daylight, it is relatively easy to spot the new ice, which shows up in dark patches. Far more dangerous is older ice that has been worn away from below by rip tides—very fast currents that sweep round headlands and along certain stretches of the coast. Since it is indistinguishable from the surrounding firm ice, its position cannot be predicted by studying a map, and one can only rely on intuition or prior knowledge to guess where to watch out for it.

I once made a week-long journey in mid-February up the length of the Thule district. The trip graphically illustrated for me the problems that can confront the arctic traveller at this time of year. I was inspired to make this expedition of over 300 miles by the fact that the sun, on its return, does not reappear simultaneously in all the district's settlements. Creeping up from the equator, its light reaches the northernmost settlement of Siorapaluk at noon a full seven days after it first shows itself at Savigsivik in the south. Watching its first rising over the sea-ice outside Savigsivik, where I was staying at the time, I realized that I could, by travelling north at the same pace

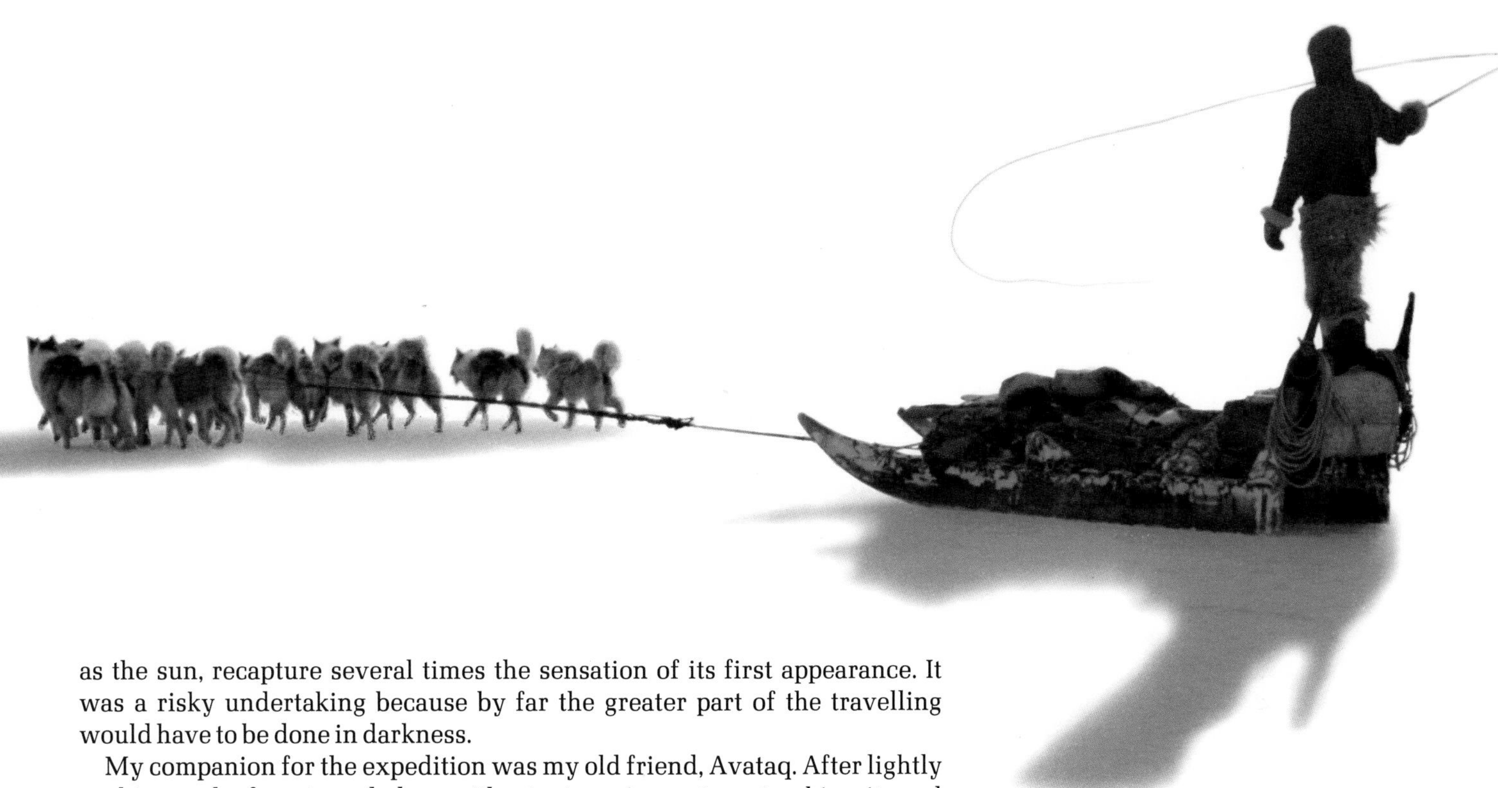

as the sun, recapture several times the sensation of its first appearance. It was a risky undertaking because by far the greater part of the travelling would have to be done in darkness.

My companion for the expedition was my old friend, Avataq. After lightly packing each of our two sledges with a tent, a primus stove, tea, biscuits and hunting equipment, we happily set out together soon after 6 a.m. on a cold, dark February morning. It was an easy enough ride at first over ice that was flat and wind-polished. Avataq several times turned away from the shoreline to look without success for seals along the edge where the fast ice met the sea. The temperature that day was far below zero and since the sea was much less cold—around the freezing-point—we could see, when the sun made a brief, midday appearance, a smoke rising from it into the bitter air. Indicating that new ice is forming in open water, the vapour is extinguished as soon as the first gossamer-thin sheet of ice seals off the sea.

We spent the first night of the trip in the hunters' hut at Cape York—one of several communal shelters scattered along the main sledging routes of the district. The next morning, our sledges swallowed up the miles; we had already seen the sun rise and set at midday before, that afternoon, we were subjected to the first real trial of our journey. Following several diversions to get round areas of broken new ice, we reached the vicinity of Parker Snow Bay, some parts of which are notoriously dangerous because of the rip tide beneath the ice. We were racing along when, abruptly, my sledge lost momentum. I realized at once that I was on old, thin ice. In such a situation, the only thing to do is to make a U-turn to get back to the safer ice as fast as possible. Avataq, who was off to one side of me, was evidently performing the same manoeuvre, to judge from the frantic shouts and whip-cracks coming from his direction. I switched on my flashlight to see what was happening, but turned it off again almost immediately, because what I saw was far worse than my imaginings. The dogs were breaking through the ice at every step and sea water was bubbling out of the holes they made. The sledge tracks were an even more alarming sight: water had seeped into them so that they looked like two jet-black lines of cold sea sweeping in a curve.

It took us five minutes to cover the few hundred yards back to firm ice. We were both somewhat shaken by the adventure. If either team had slowed down or stopped in its retreat, we would have broken through the surface, and Avataq and I, together with our sledges and huskies, would have been swallowed up in the soft mush of saturated snow that blankets the sea beneath the disintegrating crust of ice. To prevent a repetition of the incident, for the rest of the day we halted our sledges every few hundred yards and got off to probe the surface with ice-picks.

We spent that night on the north side of the desolate Pitugfik Glacier, in a rock-cave where for generations Eskimos on long journeys have sheltered. Despite our fatigue, we were too tense to fall asleep at once. I whiled away the hours listening to Avataq's stories about the experiences of previous travellers who had stayed in that very cave. While the dogs whimpered and growled outside, and the sea-ice creaked and groaned against the firm, inshore ice, he recounted a tale of a polar bear that had lumbered into the cave to find shelter from a storm. It had lain down and slept peacefully alongside the hunters who were already inside. Another more probable story involved a bear that had literally stumbled over a sleeping hunter in the cave's confined space, so terrifying the hunter and itself that man and bear had pushed their way out of the entrance together and fled in different directions.

The next two days' travel presented few difficulties because our path lay over firm sea-ice. One day we celebrated the sun's return with friends in a hunter's shack at Narssârssuk, over mugs of tea and a snack of boiled walrus meat. The next noon saw us in the village of Moriussaq, where we again joined old acquaintances in greeting the year's first rays of sunlight. It was a cheerful reunion, and the sun was long gone before we left the village to head northwards up Granville Fiord. We spent that night at the head of the fiord in a filthy little communal hut that was littered with the garbage left behind by previous travellers and damp with melted snow that had seeped through the leaky wooden roof.

The following morning, we confronted the worst stretch of our journey: the hazardous overland trek across Steensby Land, the natural barrier that lies athwart the district's main north-south sledging route. We spent the whole day in a hard haul up the glacier leading to the summit pass. Mounting the frozen slopes with a loaded sledge is difficult at the best of times. When the snow covering has been blown off by high winds, exposing the blue ice beneath, dogs and sledges are unable to keep their grip and fatal accidents can easily occur if the sledges slide out of control.

The sun briefly appeared at midday, but we had to make the latter part of the ascent in gathering twilight and it was pitch-dark by the time we reached the summit. From our vantage point 2,500 feet up, we could see the lights of Qânâq, 24 miles away across Inglefield Sound.

Avataq wanted to continue our journey but I, being tired and cold, insisted that we camp on the pass and wait until morning to make the treacherous

While his travelling companion scans the frozen sea of Melville Bay for signs of seal, a young hunter celebrating the return of the sun indulges in an exuberant handstand during a brief halt on a spring hunting trip.

descent. This decision was totally alien to Avataq's way of thinking. The Polar Eskimos have a horror of camping on a col—not unreasonably, since high cols can serve as funnels that turn strong winds into roaring hurricanes capable of sweeping away all tents in their path. Hunters will avoid these spots even when the weather is clear, as it was that night. After a few hours of fitful rest, during which every zephyr of a breeze caused Avataq to sit bolt upright, we struck a ridiculous compromise and set off by moonlight, well in advance of the first dim light of morning.

The descent was a nightmare. The normal route down the glacier had been swept clear of snow to expose a glazed surface of rippled blue ice, so we were forced to take a route down a snow-filled gully to the west of the main glacier. Only by the constant use of rope brakes and chains looped under the runners were we able to prevent the sledges from plunging headlong down the steep slope and maiming or killing the dogs. At the gully's foot, we were confronted by a terminal moraine—a ridge of rock and debris carried down the slope by the glacial ice and then left there as a 30-foot-high barrier when the glacier receded. It took us two hours of back-breaking toil to drag the sledges over it. We then had to spend a further two hours filing the sledge runners to smooth out the gouges that the sharp rocks had made in them. The sun rose and set on our labours and it was a few minutes before midnight when we finally arrived in Qânâq, where we spent the night. By the time we reached Siorapaluk the following day, we were utterly exhausted. But we had completed the 345-mile journey in seven days, according to plan, and from that point on we left the sun to continue northwards without us.

The weeks before the coming of the spring equinox in mid-March are a time of unstable weather conditions that can change dramatically from day to day. Blizzards are more common than at any other time of the year. Most dreaded of all are the warm Föhn winds that sweep down from the ice-sheet at terrifying speeds. Named after the Latin word *favonius*—the name of a warming wind—they are a common occurrence in many mountainous parts of the world and are especially prevalent on the northern slopes of the Alps. But nowhere do they occur with more violence than in northern Greenland. I have been caught on the sea-ice many times while being buffeted by such gales, which can reach astonishing speeds. On one terrible occasion I was hit by one of these winds at twilight while travelling with my wife and another companion. We were forced to spend the night lying flat beneath a tent, itself laid flat on the ice and anchored down with steel pitons and our sledges. We later heard that the wind's speed was recorded, at one of the remote weather stations in the hills behind the Thule Air Base, at 207 miles an hour—at the time, the second-highest wind velocity ever registered in the world.

Fortunately, though, the Föhn winds seldom come more than once every spring and the spells of bad weather give the hunters a respite before beginning the longer journeys ahead. Hunting in late February is still largely a matter of stalking seal and walrus at their breathing-holes. As the light returns, however, it becomes increasingly common for hunters to go out not only for one day at a time, but on two or three-day trips. On these excursions, they may spend the nights in a hut or a tent. Very occasionally, they may build themselves a snow house for overnight shelter. Perhaps because of the limited snowfall in the Thule district, the traditional igloo—a Western word derived from the Eskimo term for any kind of dwelling—was never as common among the Polar Eskimos as it was with the Eskimos of Canada. Nowadays, it is rare indeed for a hunter to construct one.

In expectation of these longer expeditions, in the weeks after the sun's return, most hunters are busy repairing their sledges and hunting gear. After a winter's wear, their equipment is usually badly in need of repair, so the months of February and March are a traditional time for overhauling tackle.

The sledge is a hunter's prime concern at any season. Each consists of a wooden platform lashed to parallel wooden runners plated with iron or nylon. At the back, twin uprights up to three feet high offer grips to make the vehicle easier to manhandle through difficult terrain. Most hunters own two sledges of different sizes: one about 10 feet in length, the other a few feet longer. The latter models are preferred for protracted trips because they ride easier over rough ice and allow more room for gear and spoils of the hunt.

A well-made sledge will last for years, but from time to time it needs attention to keep it in good order. A conscientious hunter will check carefully each day to ensure that the lashings are still secure. In the past, the Polar Eskimos used strips of bearded sealskin, which—because they were strong and slightly elastic—could be tightened up easily. Sealskin, however, is edible; and if his dogs were very hungry, a hunter could wake up in the morning to find his sledge a pile of wood lying on the ice. So now the most common material is nylon cord. But whatever material is used, the lashings tend to work loose with repeated use and they must be tightened, often simply by banging a wedge of wood between the cord and the sledge.

Other minor repairs might include fixing damaged uprights or mending cracks in the bodywork of the sledge by attaching a piece of wood or metal across the gap. The dogs' harnesses and the traces that link the team to the sledge may also need repair and replacing. Huskies tend to chew them, so tough materials are imperative: tubular nylon or military webbing are generally preferred for the harnesses, and nylon rope for the traces.

In addition, the hunter's essential weaponry may need some attention. Besides his rifle, each man will own several harpoons of different kinds, the structure varying with the purpose for which the weapon is intended. There are two main types. Those used for ice-hunting have foreshafts permanently lashed to their shafts, and detachable heads that remain embedded in the quarry after a successful assault. For summer kayak-hunting, however, the Eskimos use harpoons whose entire foreshafts detach when a harpooned prey dives. The main shaft, attached to the foreshaft by the harpoon line, remains on the surface of the water as a drag.

Once the weather allows, the Eskimos lose little time in putting their sledges to use. Hunting, however, may not be the first objective. Many men, bored with the company of the fellow-villagers with whom they have wintered, take their families to visit relatives elsewhere in the district, for the pleasure of exchanging news and stories. One of their greatest joys is sitting and listening to the adventures of others and being drawn, with a great show of reluctance, into telling a few of their own.

At this time of year, the hunters tend to gravitate to the district's administrative centre, Qânâq, partly because supplies laid in at the small village stores the previous summer are beginning to run low and partly because many have relatives living there. The annual pilgrimage to Qânâq reaches a peak at Easter, when Polar Eskimos from all over the district gather to attend services in the town's Lutheran church—the only one in the area to be served by an ordained minister. Only in these weeks does Qânâq have as many hunters in the town as there are children, old folk, Danes, and those Eskimos who have forsaken the tougher traditional life for the ease and security of a salaried job. Qânâq—with its hospital, its school, and its boiler house that provides central heating for some of the regimented lines of houses—is far from being a typical Polar Eskimo settlement. The way of life of its citizens, too, is less distinctive than that of the villagers; but this is not to suggest that it is lacking in interesting characters of its own. There are, in fact, a great many of them, but you must look for them in the hunters' quarter of the town: the rash of huts and shacks down by the frozen beach where each home has an atmosphere unique to the occupants who have created it.

On my last visit to Qânâq, I made a point of going to one tiny dwelling to see an old woman of great charm and dignity named Amaunalik, for whom I had always had a special affection. The years had treated her kindly. Although she claimed not to know her own age, her memories of past incidents dated her birth to 1907 as accurately as the rings of a tree. She was a living and intensely proud link with the past; for she traced her descent through her grandmother Itugssarssuat to Qitdlarssuaq, one of the most famous of Eskimo shamans, a folk-hero whose very existence might now be questioned by sceptics were there not evidence from independent observers to verify it.

Qitdlarssuaq did not belong to the Thule district. He was a Canadian Eskimo from Baffin Island, off Canada's northern coast. In the mid-19th century, when he was in his prime, Canadian Eskimos had not communicated with those of Greenland for generations—perhaps for as long as 300 years. But Qitdlarssuaq was a shaman; and, so story-tellers say, he learnt of the existence of his fellow-Eskimos during a trance-induced soul journey across the sea. More prosaic commentators have suggested that he heard of their existence from European whalers or explorers. What is certain is that in 1856 Qitdlarssuaq set out from Arctic Bay, his native village on Baffin Island, on a seven-year voyage across the frozen seas by way of Ellesmere Island to the Greenland coast, and that he persuaded his entire community of 38 people to go with him. According to legend, Qitdlarssuaq's spiritual might was so great that a white flame burned above his head to guide his followers at night. Travelling only in the spring, his party spent the summers in settled camps, and each winter built stone-and-turf houses in which to pass the

An Explorer's Vain Hope

On April 6, 1909, Robert Edwin Peary, a wiry, 53-year-old U.S. naval engineer, fulfilled a lifetime's ambition by reaching the North Pole. Travelling with him were his black man-servant and four Polar Eskimos. It was a fitting culmination to 18 years of collaboration between the explorer and the people of the Thule district, whom Peary later described as "my uncontaminated, pureblooded, vigorous, faithful little tribe."

Convinced that the secret of successful arctic exploration lay in exploiting Eskimo skills and equipment, Peary had made the Thule district his base for four previous expeditions from 1891 onwards. The Eskimos provided him with sledges, dog teams, fur clothing, freshly killed game—and also the expert drivers and guides needed to reach the Pole.

In exchange, Peary helped to improve the Eskimos' material well-being. When he had first arrived in the district, Peary found its inhabitants living in stone-and-turf houses, and using weapons and tools made from the only materials available: bone, hide, stone and driftwood. When he finally left them in 1909, many were equipped with rifles, telescopes, steel knives and sewing needles, canvas for tents and timber to build better sledges.

Over the years, Peary published studies of Polar Eskimo ethnology and, in order to raise funds for his expeditions, gave hundreds of lectures. He illustrated his talks with hand-tinted lantern slides, several of which, flawed with age, are shown here. In his talks he consistently expressed the hope that the Eskimos would be left in peace, "undisturbed by efforts to understand the white man's ideas of God, of right, of morality, and uncontaminated by his vices and diseases." But, ironically, the publicity he gave them brought the Polar Eskimos to the attention of the world, and so helped to expose them to the very influences that Peary feared.

Dressed from head to foot in fur garments made by Polar Eskimos, the explorer Robert Peary, then 53 years old, looks out from the bridge of the Roosevelt—the 614-ton steamship he had designed to help mount his expeditions to the North Pole.

A whaling steamer lies locked in pack ice after delivering fuel and food stocks for one of Peary's expeditions. The whaleships that delivered Peary's supplies were reinforced with double-planked, iron-plated bows so that they could break through the frozen waters. Even so, in 1893, one supply vessel, the SS Falcon, spent eight days butting at the ice before she could put into harbour.

Armed with a rifle given to him by Peary, a hunter stalks caribou on tundra strewn with arctic poppies. Within 30 years of Peary's arrival, over-shooting brought caribou to extinction in north-west Greenland.

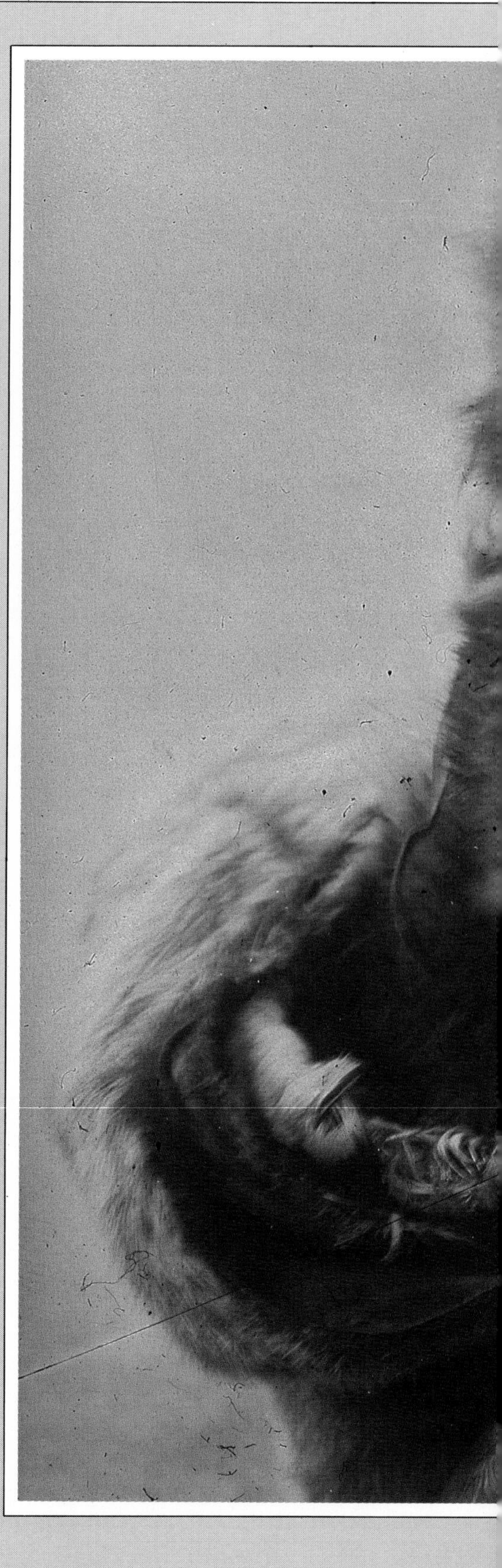

Hunters and their dogs haul one of Peary's sledges up a steep ridge of ice during his 1909 expedition to the Pole. The explorer had made two previous attempts to reach the Pole; both failed because of bad weather.

In this rare portrait-study—the fragile glass of the slide now cracked—an Eskimo baby, dressed in soft furs, perches snugly in the wide hood of its mother's sealskin jacket. Peary, who greatly admired the sewing skills of the Eskimo women, wrote, "They are more adept than any of the furriers of civilization."

four-month polar night. After two years in the arctic wilderness, some of his companions turned back home in despair. But a hardy group of 16—among them his great-granddaughter, the young Itugssarssuat—persevered. Their patience and their courage were rewarded. They finally reached Thule district, to the astonishment of the local people.

At the time of their arrival, the Polar Eskimos were at a low ebb. Under pressure of famine and disease, their population had shrunk; an explorer who visited the Eskimos in 1855 described their sorry state and counted only 140 souls. Many of their old skills had been lost with the death of the hunters who had practised them. They had even lost the art of kayak-building, and so faced hunger during the normally abundant summer months. To this demoralized group Qitdlarssuaq and his companions brought fresh blood and an infusion of new ideas. They reintroduced the kayak, and taught their hosts how to build their snow houses with tunnelled entrance passageways below ground level; because hot air rises, these ingenious entrances excluded draughts and trapped warmth inside the homes.

Qitdlarssuaq remained in the Thule district for six years. Then, as old age crept up on him, he became homesick and set off for Canada with most of his old companions—only to die the following winter on the journey home. His followers, leaderless and faced with starvation, returned to Thule and settled—this time for good. Their presence reinforced the new ideas brought by Qitdlarssuaq to Thule, and his memory is to this day still fresh among the people—now about 750 strong—whom he had done so much to aid.

Itugssarssuat was among those who stayed on. Living to the ripe old age of 84, she passed on to her granddaughter a rich repertoire of myths and folk tales, which Amaunalik had treasured and committed to memory. I have recorded many of Amaunalik's stories, often sitting at her feet beside her daughter, Tornge. With dignity, the old lady would recite—in her soft, expressive, almost magical voice—tales recalling the world that existed before the white man and his religion impinged on Polar Eskimo ways. It was a world in which starvation was a real threat and every deed had to be measured against the single question of survival.

"One of our forefathers," she would begin, clearing her throat with the customary and expected show of embarrassment at attracting her audience's attention, "one of our forefathers, it is told, when he was starving used to go out waiting at a seal's breathing-hole. One day his wife, fearing that he would eat her if he returned empty-handed, stuffed her sealskin jacket with grass and laid it in her sleeping-place. And then, it is told, she hollowed out a cave nearby as a hiding-place. Later, when she had hidden herself in the cave, her husband came home and, thinking it was his wife lying in her sleeping-place, he stabbed the sealskin jacket. Finding that it was quite without a human being, he began to boil water. And when it was boiling, it is told, he cut off a piece of his thigh and began to cook it. Then he cried out because he realized he was dying, while in the pot his thigh was boiling!"

"Ajor! What a pity!" Amaunalik would exclaim at the end of each such gruesome story. Then, looking round at her audience, she would burst into

Preparing for the long-range journeys that are possible in spring, the hunter Itukusuk smooths the nylon bands on the wooden runners of his sledge to remove dents that would slow his progress. For travel over soft terrain, nylon is now preferred to iron, since nylon is less likely to stick and pick up lumps of snow. On smooth ice, where a firm grip is needed, Itukusuk relies on a second sledge equipped with iron-shod runners.

one of the most sweet-sounding and rippling laughs I have ever heard. I never really knew whether the indignities that men heap upon themselves struck her as ridiculous, or whether she was touched by embarrassment at the effect her stories invariably had on her audience. Nevertheless, so infectious was this sound that soon everyone would be laughing; and not until the hilarity had spent itself and the room once again was silent would she clear her throat politely and start another, similar tale.

Amaunalik had many stories to tell. Where the facts ended and the fantasy began, she could not say. Whether legends, myths or true reports, never in the course of repetition did she alter a single word. She claimed merely to be the echo of history, the voice of the past. She allowed herself no licence in elaborating a tale: if a story was not repeated exactly as she had first heard it, the truth, she thought, would be lost forever.

Few of the Polar Eskimos could match Amaunalik's skill or integrity as a story-teller; yet a good number of them—then and now, men and women alike—have their own favourite tales to add to the repertoire of their people. The stories generally deal with hunting or family matters. Very occasionally they may touch on the old pre-Christian beliefs held before the missionaries arrived early in the present century. Though they seldom admit it, many Polar Eskimos are still conscious of the animistic faith of the past. In pre-Christian days, each individual was believed to consist of three distinct elements: a body, a spirit and a name. The spirit survived after the body's death in a kind of paradise. Opinions varied as to where this paradise was located; some held that it was on the moon, while others thought that it lay at the bottom of the sea. In addition, each person was said to have a second spiritual force within him, and this was invested in the name he was given. After the individual's death, the name was thought to remain behind on earth in a state of torment unless it was bestowed upon a new-born child. The act of creating a namesake enabled the name to re-enter the world of the living by a form of reincarnation. It also implied that the child who received the name of the dead person would inherit certain of his characteristics, so only those personalities who had been admired during their lifetimes could expect to be thus honoured—and their name saved.

Once, when I was alone with Avataq, he told me a story he regarded as the most certain proof that he had ever heard of the truth of reincarnation. An old woman named Ivalo and her family, he said, were staying in an igloo in Parker Snow Bay one winter when an avalanche came down from the hills with a terrible roar and crushed the snow house. The whole family managed to dig their way out, with the exception of the old woman. Her body was not recovered until the following spring, when the snow began to melt and some hunters' dogs, attracted by the scent of flesh, drew their masters to it. The old woman's right arm and shoulder were protruding from the snow. It was a horrible sight, for the gulls had pecked away all the flesh from the shoulder to the wrist. But the strange thing about this tragedy, according to Avataq, was that during the same spring a granddaughter of the old woman was born—and it was discovered that she had a birthmark that looked like a scar

Using his teeth to tighten a knot, an Eskimo hunter secures a new tip to the end of his 25-foot-long sealskin whip. The 4-foot tip, also made of sealskin, is cut much thinner than the rest of the lash so that it cracks sharply when the hunter flicks the whip. Because they are so fine, the tips wear out quickly and need frequent replacement.

running from her right shoulder down to her wrist. Everyone immediately assumed that the child was her own grandmother reborn and consequently she in turn was given the name Ivalo.

Among the men, few stories are as popular as those about the foreign visitors who find their way to the Thule district. Ever since the pioneering polar expeditions of Frederick Cook and Robert Peary at the turn of the century, Polar Eskimos have been used as guides by explorers of northern Greenland. Cook himself used the services of 17 Polar Eskimos in his assault on the North Pole, while Peary on his last two expeditions took a total of 89 Eskimos northwards with him. Women gave birth on the journeys, and little children aged five and six walked hundreds of miles through the ice and snow.

Over the last 30 years, Polar Eskimos have been employed by a new band of modern-day explorers as guides and cargo-carriers on journeys towards the Pole and over less exacting routes within their own territory. At a time of the year when they should have been hunting, they have accepted money and gone along with the adventurers for two reasons: they cannot resist the temptation of being part of a living saga, and they know they will thereafter be able to amuse themselves with tales of the follies and misadventures of their travelling companions. Although the Polar Eskimos are generally polite and hospitable towards their visitors, in private they never miss an opportunity to tease or ridicule a foreigner who presumes to travel with them.

The stories they spin of these interlopers, like all the others, seldom vary by more than a pause for breath or a sarcastic inflection. I have heard them tell of a traveller who could not bear the smell of the dogs and who insisted on erecting a plastic windscreen at the front of his sledge to deflect the odour. I have heard of another who insisted on being carried from the sledge to his tent at the end of each day, and of a third who so irritated his companions by his inability even to take down a tent or put on his own boots that his guides silently set about digging a mock grave for him in the ice to suggest his fate. Only when the man was on the verge of panic did the hunters reveal the hole's real purpose—as a repository for the camp litter.

Although such tales accurately reflect the prevalent Eskimo attitude towards most foreign travellers in their territory, I am bound to add a note of caution. The Polar Eskimos tend to exaggerate the failings of visitors, but are much more tolerant of the foibles of their own people. If a foreign explorer's dog team breaks loose, say while he is unhitching the sledge, the sound of unrestrained Eskimo laughter can echo for miles; but if the same thing happens to an Eskimo, which it does from time to time, no one is so tactless as to pay obvious attention to the incident.

I myself have witnessed this chauvinism. While driving a dog sledge in Smith Sound one day, a travelling companion of mine broke through thin ice and for a few seconds was immersed in the sea up to his armpits. He clung to the sledge uprights and was finally dragged clear by his dogs. The incident struck the Eskimos as one of the funniest things they had seen in ages and the story was repeated for days afterwards. Never once, however, did the

An exhausted hunter catnaps during a break on a long-range hunting trip. Although it is unusual for an Eskimo to sleep during a rest-stop, halts of 20 to 30 minutes are frequent on extended journeys. They give the hunters time to brew tea and untangle their dogs' traces, and permit the huskies to bite out the pieces of ice that lodge between the pads of their paws.

Anatomy of the Sledge

For nine months of every year, while the inshore ice is frozen, the Eskimos' sole means of transport is the dog sledge. This essential vehicle must be sufficiently strong and manoeuvrable to career down steep and tortuous gullies strewn with boulders, light and fast enough to cross brittle, breaking ice and yet large enough to carry the wide variety of equipment needed for even short journeys, plus a payload of meat and skins after a successful hunting trip.

All these requirements are reflected in the sledge's elaborate design. Built of pine or ash, the sturdy frame consists of a platform of planks, about one inch thick and three feet wide, resting on parallel runners, eight inches high and 11 feet long. Alternate cross-boards are lashed down with nylon cord threaded through drill-holes in the sides of the sledge. The remaining boards—each one lashed by flexible nylon cord to the plank directly behind it—are sufficiently loose to act as shock-absorbers, lifting slightly as the sledge bumps over rough surfaces.

For speed and manoeuvrability, the runners are shod with iron or nylon bands, so that they glide easily over ice or snow. In addition, the sledge has two three-foot-high uprights at the rear so that the hunter can manhandle the sledge over especially difficult terrain.

The loading of the sledge is calculated to improve mobility and make maximum use of the available space. The heaviest item—a large wooden box containing fuel and cooking equipment—is secured at the rear; thus weighted at the back, the sledge rides high at the front and imposes less strain on the dogs. Lighter items—such as hunting gear and tools—are heaped at the front of the sledge. Soft, bulky equipment—tents, sleeping bags and clothing—is packed in the centre, providing a well-cushioned seat.

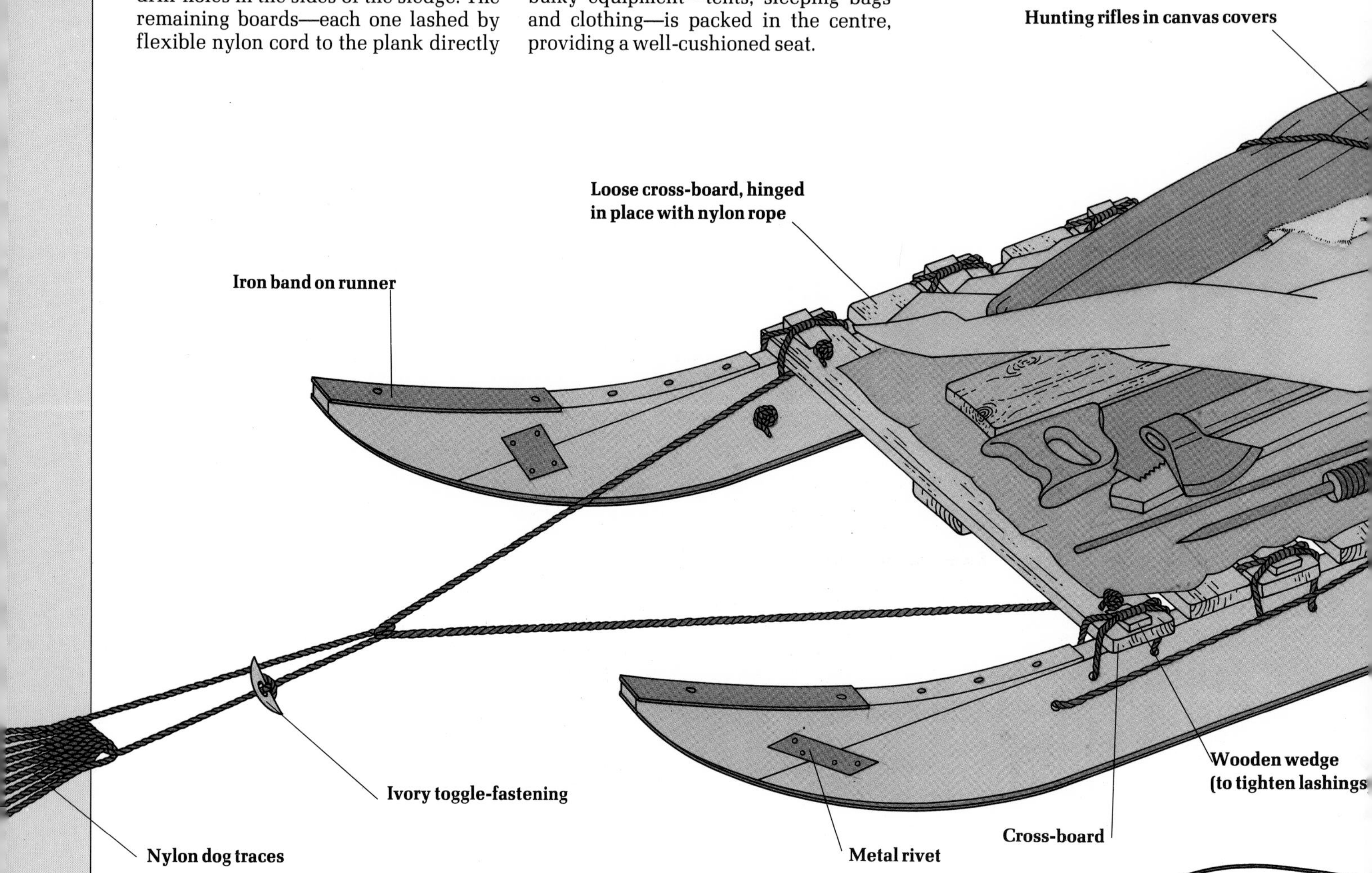

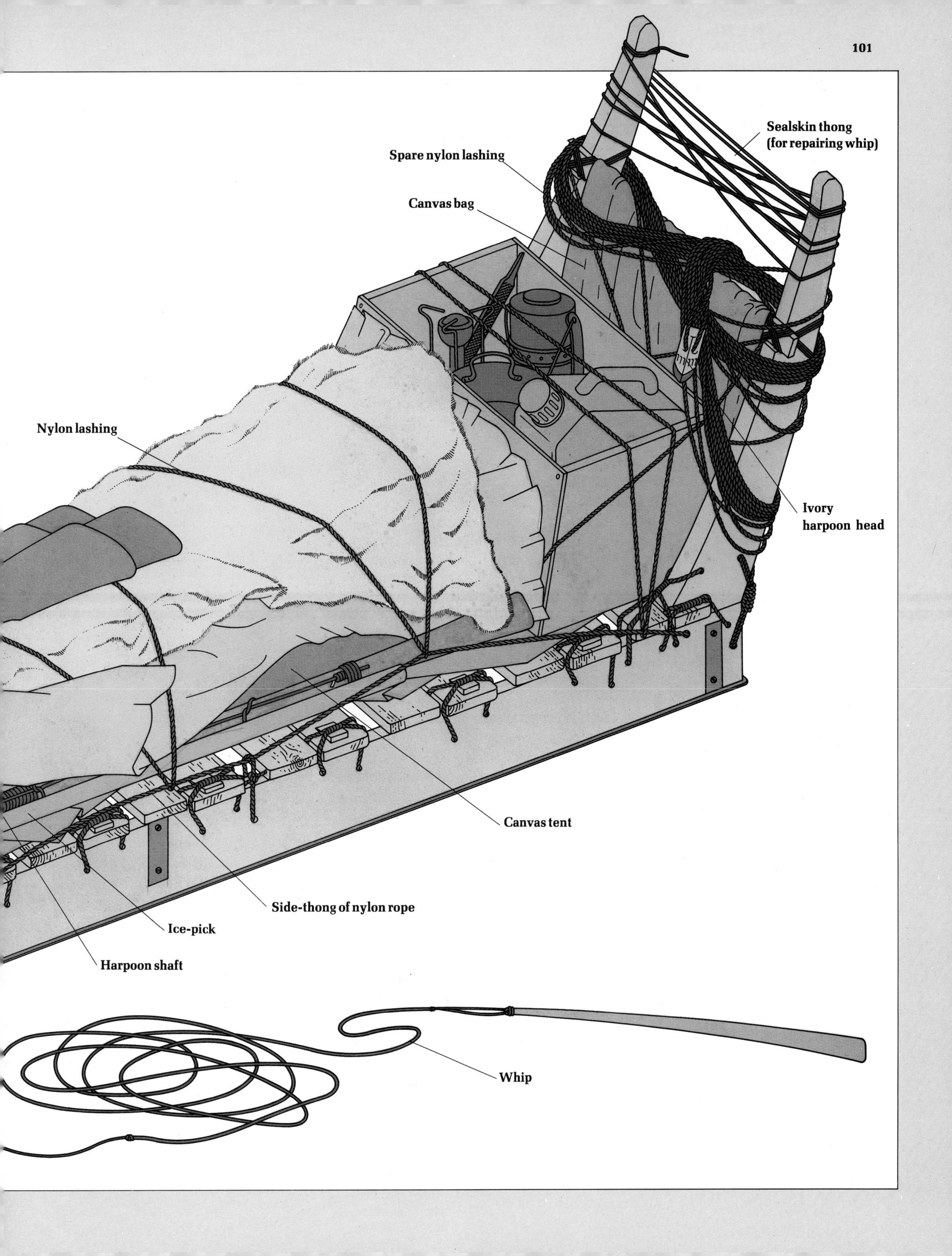
Sealskin thong
(for repairing whip)
Spare nylon lashing
Canvas bag
Nylon lashing
Ivory
harpoon head
Canvas tent
Side-thong of nylon rope
Ice-pick
Harpoon shaft
Whip

Eskimos mention that on the same day one of their own number had also broken through, lost his grip on the sledge and for several minutes splashed around in a state of panic—not unnaturally since, like most Polar Eskimos, he could not swim. He was saved from drowning by the air trapped inside his caribou parka and his polar bear-skin pants, which kept him afloat—and by a line that was thrown to him by my much-mocked companion!

In the fullness of time, however, an explorer may finally discover that he has won the respect of his guides. The Polar Eskimos show their regard in their own direct way: by treating the explorer as a competent traveller, like themselves. On one occasion, bad weather made me five days late in returning from a hazardous journey to the village of Qeqertarssuaq. My hunter friends, who were waiting with growing anxiety for my arrival in the village, came under pressure not only from the women but from most of the old men as well to go out to look for me in case I was in trouble. They flatly refused, arguing that it would be an insult to another traveller to suspect that he was in need of help. And so I was presented with the supreme irony: only my death would have proved them wrong.

By the first days of March, day and night are almost equally divided, and the tide of life returns to the hunting-grounds. The polar bears have left the mainland territories where the females give birth, and are prowling after seals along the fast-ice edge and out on the open pack ice. Also at this time, the arctic hares are mating in the coastal valleys, and female ringed seals prepare to give birth in snow caves and lairs they have hollowed out of drifts near icebergs trapped among the pack ice.

The hunters sense these happenings and suddenly become aware that the meat caches in the villages are low, and that they have spent enough time talking with friends and neighbours and building or repairing sledges. There is a sense of urgency to put more meat on their racks and more fat on their dogs. It is time again to go hunting.

At this season of the year above all others a fundamental division appears between the hunters. The great majority will still concentrate on hunting trips of three or four days. On such journeys, they will seek walrus in the water around areas of broken ice or else at breathing-holes in the patches of new ice that still form near the open sea each time the temperature lowers. Seal-hunting at breathing-holes also continues, though the thickness of the inshore ice makes the task of cutting a hole to retrieve the carcass more time-consuming. Occasionally, while the short-range hunters are out looking for other prey, there is an impromptu polar bear chase, starting with the chance discovery of bear tracks. The limit of the short-range hunters' exertions would be a 10-day trip along the edge of the pack ice, looking for either seal or walrus and hoping to pick up signs of a bear.

There are sound economic reasons for these hunters to stay close to home. By concentrating their energy and skills on accumulating saleable sealskins, fox furs, and walrus meat and ivory—all of which fetch a good cash price in the trading stores—the most successful short-range hunters can earn more

How to Build an Igloo

Nothing so vividly symbolizes the Eskimo's ingenuity in surviving his hostile world as the igloo, a snug shelter constructed entirely from blocks of firm snow. Such shelters are now rare sights in the Thule district; hunters away from home normally sleep in tents. But the protection afforded by an igloo surpasses that of any tent and hunters still occasionally build one as a secure refuge when a prolonged storm threatens.

An igloo is constructed to make maximum use of the hunter's own body heat—often supplemented by a primus stove. The snow walls and roof provide good insulation. To take advantage of the fact that warm air rises, the Eskimo positions himself not on the floor of the igloo but on a snow shelf some three feet higher. A small vent cut in the roof of the dwelling can be uncovered to lower the temperature if the igloo becomes so warm that the inner walls start to thaw.

Although thermodynamically sophisticated, an igloo is relatively simple to make: a skilled hunter can build one in three hours. He begins by locating an area of hard-packed snow and hewing out several dozen blocks for the dome.

The base of the hole excavated for the snow blocks becomes the floor of the igloo. A raised platform of untouched snow inside the hole serves as the sleeping platform. Working from the floor, the hunter lays a circle of blocks, encompassing the hole. Each block is trimmed into final fit with a knife, then tilted slightly inwards. He fits subsequent blocks in a spiral pattern, tilting each tier more sharply to create the dome. To complete the igloo, the hunter cuts a door out of two adjacent snow blocks on the leeward side of the structure at ground level, then excavates an entry trench.

The hunter Qâviganguaq uses a carpenter's saw to cut snow blocks. He needs 30 of them to make an igloo six feet in circumference and rising about three feet above ground level. Each block is about three feet long by two feet wide, and some six inches deep—just thick enough to keep out the bitter cold.

Standing in the three-foot-deep pit that will form his igloo's sunken floor, Qâviganguaq uses a knife to trim the sides of snow blocks and fit them neatly together. He must then bevel the tops of the blocks so that the succeeding layer will tilt inwards to begin the upward spiral of the igloo dome.

Having completed the walls, the hunter manoeuvres the last block through the hole at the top to cap the dome (above). He will then pack loose snow between blocks to make the walls draught-proof. Later he relaxes inside the shelter (right) on his sleeping platform beside a paraffin lamp which, together with his own body heat, will raise the temperature of the snow house more than 50°F above that of the outside air.

in a good year than the highest-paid Danish administrator in the territory.

But there are other hunters, who have strong teams of good dogs, who will set out in groups of three or four during March on polar bear hunts that will last eight weeks or more and take them perhaps into areas they have never seen before. The chosen arena for long-range bear hunters who live south of Steensby Land is generally the ice-covered expanses of Melville Bay. Those who live in the northern part of the district go up to Smith Sound and beyond. Prestige among these hunters tends to be measured by the distances they travel rather than their wealth. On a long journey, because the weight they can carry on their sledges is strictly limited, they seldom stop to kill more seal or walrus than they need to satisfy their immediate needs. Only if the hunters are following a route by which they are likely to return might they kill extra animals and cache the meat under a cairn of rocks designed to protect it from marauding bears or foxes. Normally, however, they put their trust in their skill as hunters to find game to sustain them and their dogs in the area into which they are wandering.

On several occasions I have seen such hunters, when they were several hundred miles from home, pass by a herd of walrus without dispatching a single one. In one case, my companions could have killed at least 20 walrus at the cost of no more than 20 rounds of ammunition. Had they been fortunate enough to find such a big herd a few miles from their home, they would have bagged 10 to 20 tons of meat and blubber—enough to last them right through the year, with at least five tons of spare meat that they could have sold.

One might expect the long-range hunters to curse the gods for teasing them with the sight of large herds, but instead they laugh and pass by, or stop their sledges and crawl on their bellies towards the herds, just for the fun of seeing how close they can get to the nearest bull before the whole herd starts to roar and flop and heave itself towards the nearest pool of smoking, soupy-looking sea. By this time, their minds are squarely set on polar bears and nothing can distract them.

The polar bear is now a protected species in all the arctic countries, and the Polar Eskimos are among the few people in the world who are allowed to hunt it with few restrictions. They need polar bear pelts for their pants and they use the long hairs of that pelt for trimming their wives' fox-fur pants and stockings. But there is a much more important need that drives the long-range hunters—a need that only became clear to me when I first experienced a polar bear hunt in the middle of Smith Sound. For these hardy hunters, the chase after the bears is a ritual trial of skill and courage that plunges the participants headlong into the special poetry of savage conflict.

When the bear is finally spotted, excited whisperings and pointing fingers are the prelude to the start of the chase. The lashings that hold the cargo on the hunters' sledges are immediately slashed with knives and most of each load is dumped on the ice. Within seconds, every lightened sledge is scorching the ice behind 10 or 15 dogs at full gallop, heading straight for the bear, while each rider holds on as though his very life is at stake. The hunters call to each other and urge on the dogs with the special cry they reserve for polar bear hunting: a sound that mimics the raven's call, because the birds are the traditional companions of polar bears, following them to scavenge on the scraps left after the bears have killed and consumed their prey.

As the hunters close in, they crawl forward on their careering sledges, riding them like toboggans and throwing their weight from side to side to keep from overturning as they bounce over the ice. As the hunter reaches the front of the sledge, he stretches forward to haul in, hand over hand, the traces of the galloping dogs, so that he can cut loose two or three of the fastest and fiercest dogs to bring the bear to bay. Off go the freed dogs at an incredible pace in pursuit of the bear—now in full flight towards the nearest patch of open water, where its superiority as a swimmer will enable it quickly to escape its pursuers. The dogs close the gap and the sledges, pulled by the rest of the teams, thunder after them. More dogs are let loose to support those that have now caught up with the bear and are circling it, diving at its flanks and leaping on its back. Some are knocked flying through the air; some may be slashed open by the bear's claws. One may have its skull crushed with a single blow of a giant paw.

The noise, the odours of blood and fear, build up to a climax as the hunters move in with all the dogs now loose and swarming round the bear. There is a single shot—it seems to be a dull thud of air—and the bullet hits its target. The bear, huge and magnificent, crumples into the mass of yapping dogs. The swarming animals quieten, circle the corpse, sniff at it, nip at it and then, knowing they cannot bite through the thick hide, stroll away and lie down.

I have been on scores of polar bear hunts with the Polar Eskimos. I have seen bears seek their safety on thin ice, shuffling carefully out to the point where it was thinnest and then rearing up to crash their whole weight down on it to break through to the water below. I have seen men and dogs, in their excitement, follow the bear on to that thin ice until it bent a full 18 inches under their weight—at which point the men suddenly realized their danger and, stretching themselves on to the ice, crawled back to safety—all the while sweating with fear. I have seen bears that seemed, as in a mirage, to be walking on thin air, because the ice-cooled and sun-warmed air strata of early March caused the surface on which they were standing to disappear. I have seen bears emerge from the centre of a rising sun low on the horizon, and bears that have walked right into my camp. I have blundered into bears towering above me at a range of only a few feet, so that I had time for only one shot to save my life. But never, never will I see a bear in a setting more dramatic, wild and deeply moving than in its typical last heroic stand, surrounded by a pack of dogs, as it spins and rears up trying to sweep its assailants away before the hunter dispatches it and claims his long-sought prey.

This is the Polar Eskimo hunter in his moment of ultimate glory. He needs the bear not only as a predator needs its prey, but as a challenger in contest with whom he reaffirms his prowess as a hunter and his valour as a man.

The Ultimate Quarry

When spring comes to northern Greenland, polar bears leave their breeding territories on the mainland and range far over the frozen sea to prey on seal and fish. At this time, the hunter, in turn, is hunted. Polar bears provide the fur for the Eskimos' traditional trousers; the long, dense pelt is warm, wind and water-resistant, comfortable and very durable—a combination of qualities unmatched by man-made materials. But only the best hunters and dog teams pursue this coveted and elusive quarry. To find polar bears in their vast hunting grounds, the hunters may have to endure weeks of hardship, risking injury and even death amid the treacherous ice.

One day in late March, photographer Bryan Alexander joined the hunter Itukusuk and his nephew Mamarut as they set out from the settlement of

Travelling on the thick layer of sea-ice adjoining the shoreline, dog teams pull the hunters' two sledges towards the sunset at the end of the hunt's first

Narssârssuk for a long chase in search of polar bears. Their two dog sledges were heavily loaded with supplies, hunting equipment and tents. After a rendezvous farther south with three other hunters, they turned westwards into Melville Bay. For almost three weeks, the weather was against them. Forced by a storm to retreat to the village of Savigsivik, they set out again only to run into gale-force winds that piled up ridges in their path and broke up the ice into fast-moving floes.

At last, after a circuitous 300-mile journey that took them back to within a day's travel of their starting point, they happened upon fresh tracks—the distinctive five-clawed prints of a polar bear. Their fatigue and previous disappointments erased, the hunters turned to pursue their quarry.

day. From Narssârssuk, the party followed the coast southwards to Cape York before reaching their chosen hunting ground, Melville Bay (inset map).

Outward Bound

For the first night, the hunters' destination was a sea-cliff 27 miles south of Narssârssuk that gives shelter from the strong winds that blow off the ice-sheet. Itukusuk and Mamarut had arranged to rendezvous at the cliff with Itukusuk's brother, Masauna. On arriving there, they found Masauna already camped in the lee of the cliff with his son Mikile and a companion, Panigpak.

Breaking camp early the following day, the five sledges continued down the coast to Cape York, a lofty promontory jutting southwards into Melville Bay. There, the party encountered three seal hunters who were from Savigsivik, the southernmost village in the region. The nine men spent the night at the foot of the Cape in a hunters' refuge, exchanging news and gossip until the early hours of the morning. After only a few hours of snatched sleep on a shared sleeping platform inside the hut, Itukusuk and his five companions were up, ready to start across the ice-covered bay.

The hut at Cape York (right) is one of several refuges in the Thule district built by the Eskimos for the communal use of travellers in need of temporary shelter. The hut, which lacks food and fuel, provided rough-and-ready overnight accommodation (inset, above) for Itukusuk and all his companions, who found enough space for themselves on the wooden sleeping platform.

Weathering a Storm

Within hours of the party's departure from Cape York, the weather began to deteriorate. A wind in excess of 30 m.p.h. broke up the ice into floes too far apart for the sledges to bridge. Keeping to the intact ice bordering the coastline, the hunters retreated towards Savigsivik.

The wind gathered force, reducing visibility to a few yards. But the sledges moved steadily on, and photographer Bryan Alexander noted in his journal: "The ability of Eskimos to navigate in a storm without a compass never ceases to amaze me." After five hours, the party reached Savigsivik, where, for four days, they sat out the tempest in a local hunter's house. The dog teams remained tethered outside throughout the blizzard.

During their enforced stay, the hunters were visited by an old man who demanded rum. Although Itukusuk gave him the last of their alcohol, the old man flew into a rage and placed a curse of bad weather on the hunters. Itukusuk, although visibly shaken, ignored the curse. Later he explained to Alexander that the old man was credited with possessing shamanistic powers.

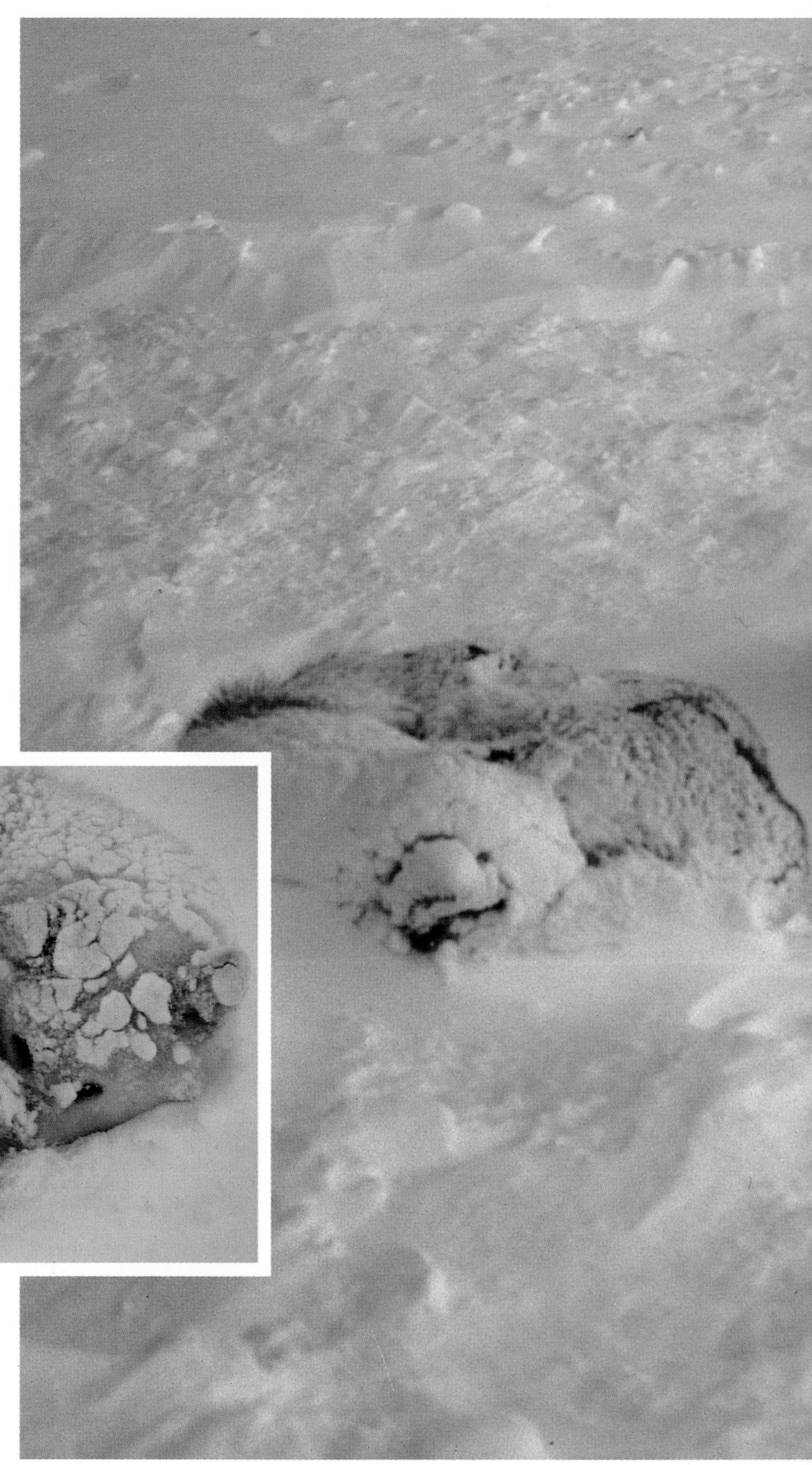

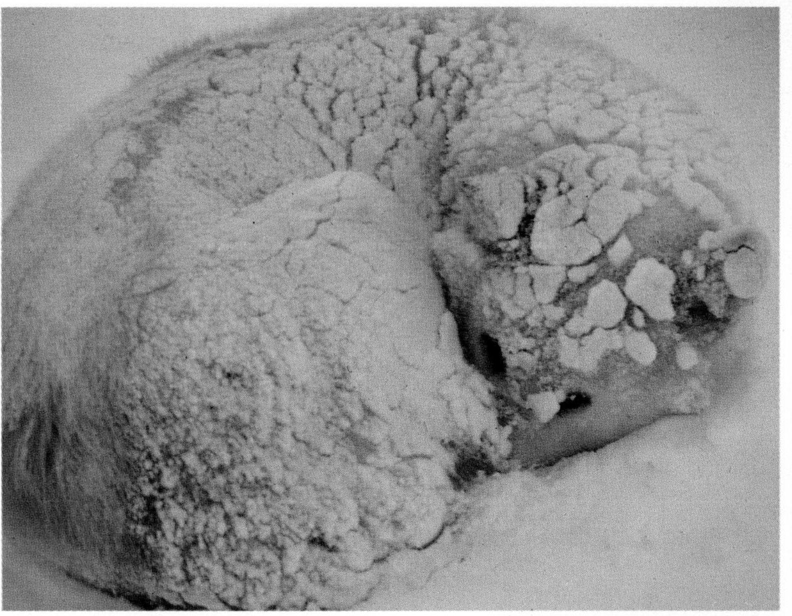

Tethered to rocks under the snow, the huskies weather the four-day storm. To conserve warmth in sub-zero temperatures, each husky curls up into a ball (inset, above), using its bushy tail to protect its sensitive nose from the danger of frost-bite.

Rough Going

On the seventh day of their trip, the party once again set out over Melville Bay. Although the weather had improved, travelling remained difficult because the winds had pushed the sea-ice—uneven at the best of times—into ridges as high as 15 feet. These obstacles not only slowed the hunters' progress almost to a standstill, but obscured their view.

To make things worse, the wind soon began to blow again, breaking up the ice. Alexander noted: "For about an hour we were adrift on a floe. We managed to reach safe ice only by moving very quickly across a series of smaller floes. Keeping together proved extremely difficult because the ice was moving so fast; no sooner had one sledge crossed than the gap between the floes widened, leaving the next sledge stranded. Masauna got separated on a floe and drifted completely out of sight before he managed to find a way back to us."

It was several hours before the party was together on firm ice, but the hunters were able to exploit their situation. They found a channel inhabited by seals and shot six to replenish the meat supplies for themselves and their five dog teams.

After the storm, one of the dog teams cautiously makes its way over the pressure ice—ridged ice created when floes are driven together by high winds. Open water between floes made progress even slower; the hunters sometimes manoeuvred their sledges over bridges made by throwing chunks of ice into the water (inset, above).

Making Camp

On the 11th day, as the hunters continued their journey over Melville Bay, still not having sighted any bears, the weather worsened again, and a wind gusting to 40 m.p.h. compelled the party to stop and make camp in the lee of an iceberg. They sat out the storm in their tents. Despite the bad weather there was much joking and horseplay between the Eskimos.

The weather remained bad on the following day, and a rumbling noise like the sound of distant thunder confirmed the hunters' fears that the wind was breaking up the ice so badly that further progress over the bay was impossible. When the next day dawned fine, they reluctantly agreed to return to land and then split into two groups for the rest of the journey. Photographer Alexander continued travelling with Itukusuk and Mamarut. After a hearty meal of boiled seal meat, the three headed north on the long journey homewards to Narssârssuk.

Canvas tents provide adequate shelter for overnight halts when no hut is near. To erect the tents, the hunters ran two sledges side by side to create a sleeping platform (inset, top), then drove harpoons into the ice to support the covering (inset, above). At night, primus stoves provided warmth and light.

Picking up the Trail

Itukusuk and his party journeyed back to Savigsivik—a trip that took 16 hours—then followed a well-used route homewards up the coast, still keeping watch for signs of bear and seal. A deep layer of new snow had fallen and the drivers had to use their whips to keep the dog teams moving. En route, they met up with other travellers who were heading north to Qânâq, Thule district's largest settlement. One of them was Jens Danielsen, a hunter from Itukusuk's village. After a friendly reunion, the neighbours joined forces for the day's journey northwards.

The opportunity the hunters had been seeking in vain for nearly three weeks finally presented itself by chance. Shortly after setting out, as they went along the sea-ice fringing the coastline, the hunters came upon fresh bear tracks. Immediately they took up the trail. The tracks led inland along an inlet, then doubled back out to sea over the pack ice. Bryan Alexander wrote: "Our chances of finding the bear seemed slim, as we could travel only slowly through the deep snow that covered the ice."

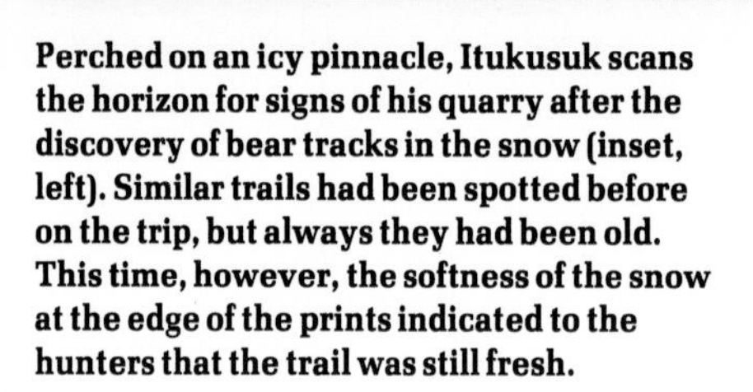

Perched on an icy pinnacle, Itukusuk scans the horizon for signs of his quarry after the discovery of bear tracks in the snow (inset, left). Similar trails had been spotted before on the trip, but always they had been old. This time, however, the softness of the snow at the edge of the prints indicated to the hunters that the trail was still fresh.

End of the Chase

For two hours the sledges followed the bear's trail, moving with painful slowness through the deep snow. To gain speed, Itukusuk, who had temporarily jettisoned much of the equipment from his sledge for extra speed, drew ahead of the other two drivers to lead the chase.

He came upon his quarry by surprise as it dozed in the shadow of an iceberg. Alerted by the barking huskies, the bear took to flight. Itukusuk cut the traces of his best three dogs, which bounded across the ice to harry the bear and keep it at bay until the other hunters arrived.

When Itukusuk came within rifle range, he fired a shot, hitting the bear in a foreleg. In a vain attempt to escape, the wounded animal plunged into a nearby channel, where Itukusuk harpooned it in the flank to prevent it from swimming to safety. Mamarut, who had followed close behind Itukusuk, finally killed it with a rifle shot. The three hunters used the harpoon line to drag the carcass clear of the water and on to firm ice, where it could be skinned and butchered.

Confronted by a snarling husky, the bear struggles to free itself from the harpoon line anchored in its body. Holding the line taut between its paws, the wounded animal unsuccessfully tried to sever it with its teeth before Mamarut finally dispatched the bear with a shot to the head (inset, right).

Under the watchful eyes of the waiting huskies, the hunters haul their prey out of the channel, using Itukusuk's harpoon line, which is looped in

a noose around the bear's neck, as a towing rope. They then set about the task of skinning it as quickly as possible, before the carcass began to freeze.

Dividing the Spoils

After the kill, the skinned bear's hide was measured with a harpoon shaft so that it could be divided up according to the traditional rules governing hunting shares. Itukusuk, who first shot the bear, took the front half of the skin and the choicest cuts of meat. Mamarut and Jens shared the remaining spoils. They rinsed the skin, then trampled it in snow to clean it of blood. There was enough bear skin to make three pairs of trousers.

With their spoils packed away on their sledges, the triumphant party returned to land and, after a celebratory meal of boiled bear meat, set out on the last leg of the journey home—15 hours away. The temperature had now dropped to –13°F. The party reached Narssârssuk at 3 a.m., exhausted and cold but in high spirits. News of their return spread quickly and, despite the late hour, neighbours crowded into Itukusuk's hut to welcome the hunters back and celebrate their exploits with rum until well after dawn.

After flaying the bear's carcass, Itukusuk stretches out the blood-stained skin on the ice to divide it among the hunters involved in the kill. After cleaning his own share, he hooked it on to the upright of his sledge and beat off loose snow with a stick to prevent it from freezing on the skin (inset, above).

As the weary dog teams return to Narssârssuk, Mamarut celebrates the approaching home-coming with whoops of glee and a wave of his arms and legs.

Four | Spell of the Summer Sun

Every spring, during their trips to the far north in search of polar bear, there comes a moment when long-range Eskimo hunters are suddenly stopped in their tracks by an almost physically painful desire to return home. I have seen this happen often, each time without warning. One day the hunter who has been away perhaps a month or more feels so completely in tune with his environment that he regards the mere thought of turning back as sacrilege. The next day, or sometimes only hours later, a strange uneasiness seizes him and all at once, often with barely a word to his companions, he will turn and head hell-bent for home, driving his dogs as though his life were at stake.

There are pragmatic reasons for this dramatic turnabout. By mid-April, the Polar Eskimo who is hunting to the north of Smith Sound becomes increasingly aware that the four-month period of continuous daylight is imminent. The sun is already above the horizon for as much as 23 hours a day, and the thaw is under way. For another seven or eight weeks, the sea-ice will remain safe for sledging. The snow covering, however, melts more quickly and, as long as the ice beneath it remains firm, there is no outlet through which the melt-water can drain off. As a result, in sheltered areas, where heavy snowfalls lie undisturbed by winds, the ice is soon covered in slush that may be knee-deep in places. Travelling conditions become appalling and remain so until some weeks later, when the first melt holes appear in the sea-ice to serve as outlets down which the melted snow can escape. Progress by dog sledge is now reduced to perhaps one mile an hour and the hunter is sometimes compelled to get behind his sledge and push while his dogs up front flounder out of their depth.

Several times, I myself have endured the nightmare of travelling through slush in early May. I have screamed myself hoarse to urge my dogs through a quagmire of saturated snow that in places resembles a milky brown soup. I have also travelled in processions in which three sledges and their dog teams were hitched together in order to sustain momentum with extra pulling-power. It made a depressing sight: a string of miserable animals, sinking

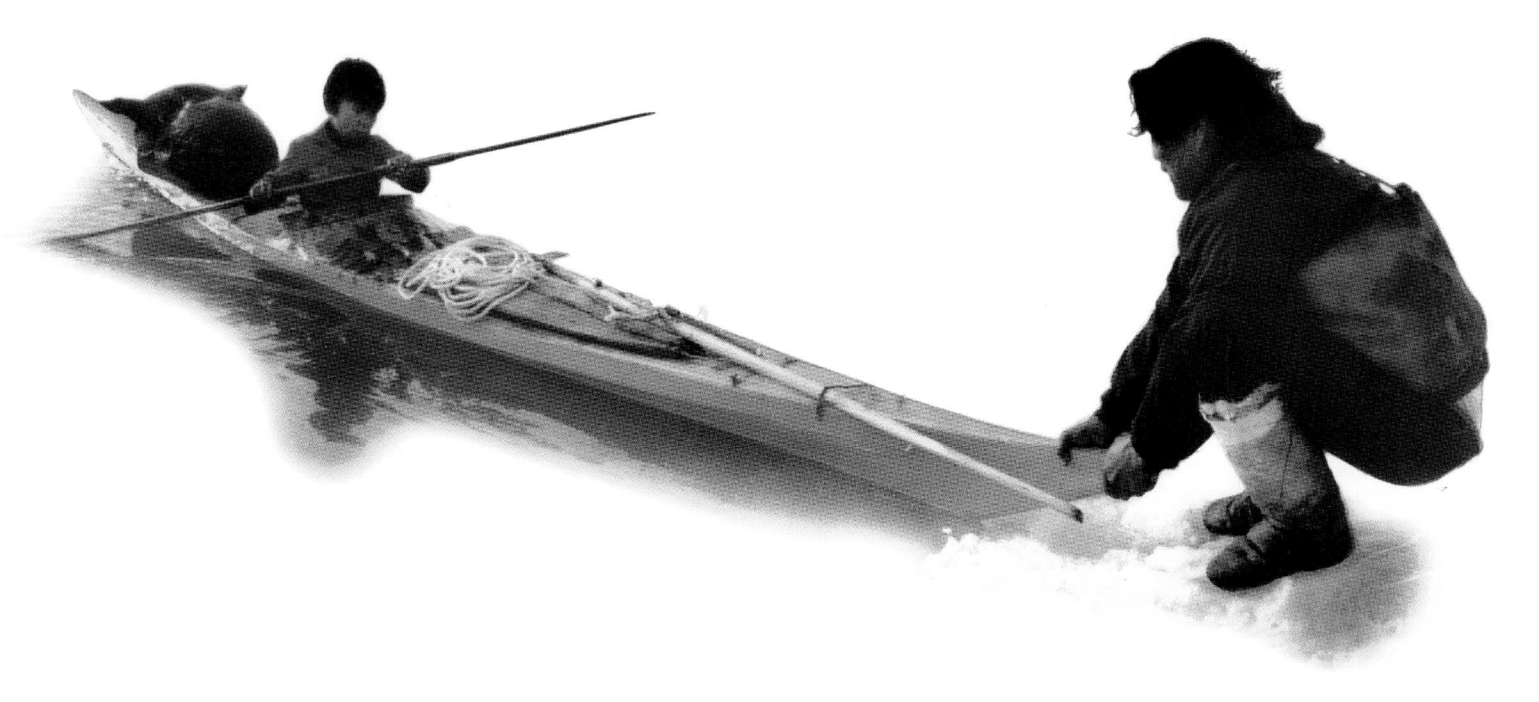

sledges and shouting men that stretched for more than 200 yards and weaved forward like a gigantic snake to avoid the melted snow that formed deep pools in every dip of the uneven sea-ice. After each such experience I have sworn I would never again get caught up in this foolish game of dicing with the weather of the arctic spring.

Yet there is little pleasure in arriving back in a village days ahead of all the other hunters. In doing so, you may have demonstrated your common sense, but something of honour is lacking. The greatest satisfaction goes to the man who times his arrival to perfection—who is neither too early nor too late. Ideally, his family will be kept in suspense until his return during the first days of summer, when the entire village will turn out to welcome him home. By custom, the first person to greet him will be his wife who, if she has an appropriate sense of occasion, will have hurriedly changed into her best clothes—a brightly coloured anorak, fox-fur pants and thigh-length white boots—at the first far-away glimpse of his sledge on the sea-ice.

At the moment of reunion, the hunter is in all probability genuinely exhausted; his fatigue after a journey of hundreds of miles is as real as the dark patches of frost-bite on his face. At the same time, he knows that he strikes a heroic figure and that his stature will be enhanced by a modest demeanour. Thus, following the rules of the game, he will never complain of the hardships he has endured. Instead, he will assume a nonchalant air to heighten the climactic moment when his wife and children unpack the sledge and utter squeals of delight on discovering the creamy white pelt of a polar bear.

It is a great moment—provided, of course, that he has indeed brought back at least one polar bear skin. But pity the lone hunter who had delayed too long. His arrival, as a bedraggled and weather-beaten figure floundering through deep slush, is likely to stir only momentary interest. By this time, the villagers have their minds on the coming season. Migratory birds of enormous variety, streaming in from the south, have brought a new dimension to the hitherto still and silent land. As the natural world around them awakes to

the sights and sounds of summer, the majority of Polar Eskimos are concerned only with preparing to leave their villages to camp in tents at various time-honoured locations that offer an abundance of good hunting. It is time to take advantage of the most pleasurable of the arctic seasons.

Summer is the one time of year that allows all the Polar Eskimos a rich and varied open-air life. The changing climate and ice conditions ensure a wide choice of game; and for this one season the hunter's entire family often get the chance to accompany him on his expeditions. The children are on holiday from school; and the wives too are generally eager to escape from the houses to which they have been confined for much of the year. There is little risk of monotony. If a hunter tires of one form of hunting, he can soon switch to another. And, if he and his family become sick of the company in one camp, they can always pack up their tents and move on.

The great thaw is gradual and sporadic, despite the continuous daylight, and each stage brings a different type of hunting. In May and early June, when the sun is still low in the sky at midnight, the average temperature is just above the freezing-point. Out to sea, the ice-edge is slowly retreating towards the coast; but the inshore ice is still firm enough to bear the weight of sledges. During these weeks, the hunter may stalk seal as they bask in the sun on the ice, or take a boat to hunt walrus that are lazing on ice-floes near points and promontories where the sea-ice has been swept out by early summer winds. Alternatively, he can take his family to cliffs or coastal hills to net little auks now breeding in their millions.

Later in June, the thawing accelerates sharply, yet sea conditions vary so dramatically with the effect of winds and currents that it is possible to approach an island off the coast by dog sledge on one side and leave it by boat from an opposite shore. Only at the end of July—some five or six weeks after Midsummer's Day, when the temperature has settled at around 40°F—does the Thule district finally become largely free of ice. New hunting possibilities again open up. There are char to be caught in some of the lakes and streams; more importantly, the hunter can go out in his kayak to harpoon narwhal, which venture into the fiords at this time of year to calve and feed.

High summer—the time when the majority of days are warm and clear—extends only through July and the first half of August. Polar Eskimos, however, undeterred by the prospect of icy winds and sudden snow storms, are always eager to set out for summer hunting sites as early as the third week of May. They treat these camping trips as a kind of working holiday. Besides good hunting, the camps provide a new social environment as families from different villages suddenly find themselves to be neighbours.

Furthermore, they are glad to be quit of their permanent home at a time when day by day, the villages are becoming less inviting. In late May, melting snow drips off rooftops, pools of slush yellow with dog urine appear between the houses, rubbish dumps exposed by the sun begin to foul the air, and children who have been playing outdoors are perpetually coming home with their clothes soaking wet and the soles of their boots caked with muddy

Concealed behind a shooting-screen set on sledge-like runners, a hunter slides towards his prey: a basking seal. Having dispatched his target with a rifle shot, he retrieves the carcass (inset, right), moving gingerly over the thin ice near the seal's breathing hole.

slush or canine excrement. Only the very old and the infirm are prepared to stay at home throughout the summer, although in extended periods of inclement weather wives often wait in the village while their husbands hunt.

In late May, in every village, you see entire families—children, parents and grandparents—moving out on sledges piled high with tents, hunting equipment, bedding, primus stoves, cans of kerosene, pots and pans, coffee, tea and biscuits, battered suitcases and wooden boxes stuffed with clothes, plus perhaps various treasured possessions that members of the family have surreptitiously added to the load when the hunter was not looking. Perched precariously on top of everything are the children—a little girl clutching her favourite doll, a small boy jealously guarding new-born puppies that peep out of a carrier bag, and older offspring noisily celebrating the prospect of three full months of adventure and freedom from school. And somewhere under this moving mass will be at least one of the hunter's boats—a kayak or, sometimes now, a motor-powered boat of wood or fibreglass.

The kayak—a one-man canoe—is still standard equipment for the Polar Eskimo hunter. The frame is traditionally constructed of small pieces of wood, then covered with canvas or sealskin. In length, each kayak—tailored to the hunter—is about three times his height. Its circular hold, slightly aft of centre, is cut to fit his proportions. Propelled by a double-bladed wooden paddle, it skims across the sea, silent, arrow-straight, and sufficiently low in the water for the harpoon-bearing hunter in it to lean forward and conceal his approach behind large pieces of drifting ice. On calm seas it is the perfect craft in which to creep up on seal and narwhal.

But the kayak, so light and so frail, has obvious limitations. It can easily be capsized or damaged—especially by an angry walrus. Also, paddling it over great distances is tiring. So the hunters have equal need of boats powered by small motors, which they buy from the Royal Greenland Trade Department store in Qânâq. The motor boats permit travel in summer far over the sea and hunting at greatly reduced risk in waters strewn with the ice-floes on which walrus are commonly found.

The respective advantages of the kayak and motor boat were impressed upon me during one of the summers I spent on Herbert Island, hunting with Avataq and his two teenage sons. We spent June at a camp at the western end of the island where we could hunt walrus in open waters from motor boats. In July we used Avataq's home village of Qeqertarssuaq as our base, then, towards the end of the month, we moved to the island's eastern tip, facing Inglefield Sound, where we used the kayaks to hunt narwhal coming into the ice-free fiord.

First, however, I was introduced by Avataq to a very different kind of hunting. We spent several days engaged in one of the most popular and fruitful activities that the late-May combination of sunshine and sea-ice affords: stalking seal after they have hauled themselves up through holes in the ice to lie basking in the sunshine.

The hunter first locates such prey by scanning the sea-ice with binoculars from a high vantage point. He sledges to within a few hundred yards of his

A young girl and boy, still wearing their traditional winter garb of polar bear-skin trousers and sealskin boots, play a one-on-one game of tug-o'-war to celebrate the coming of summer. With the start of the long school holidays at the end of May, Eskimo children of all ages are free to accompany their parents to outdoor hunting camps.

quarry, then proceeds on foot. The art lies in approaching the seal unobserved: to remain hidden, the hunter crouches, and later crawls, behind a shooting-screen. The screen is like a small, square-rigged sail of white linen that is stretched tight and set on two runners wrapped in sealskin or polar bear hair to muffle the sound of its movement. The hunter's rifle is poked through an aperture in the centre of the screen that is just large enough to allow him to see along his sights.

Of course, it is possible to shoot a seal from a distance without using a screen as camouflage. But there is always the chance that the animal will only be wounded, surviving long enough to slither away through its hole in the ice. The best strategy, therefore, is to get within a range of 50 yards or so and be fairly sure of killing the seal instantly with a shot through the brain. Such proximity also enables the hunter, if necessary, to dash forward after shooting and grab a wounded seal before it slips back into the sea.

This form of hunting is complicated by the fact that the seal, always wary of attack by a polar bear, seldom sleeps for more than one minute at a time. It constantly raises its head to look around; and every time it does so, the advancing hunter must stop and remain absolutely still behind his shooting-screen. To improve his camouflage, the hunter makes sure that the sun is not behind him, because its light would silhouette him against the screen. As an added precaution, he may wriggle forward on his elbows for the last 50 yards or so of his approach, gaining extra cover from any hummock of ice that lies between himself and the seal.

Long ago, when Polar Eskimo hunters went out on to the ice armed only with harpoons, seal-stalking was an art demanding extraordinary patience and perseverance since the odds were very much in the seal's favour. It still requires skill. But now the rifle has given the hunters a definite advantage. Consequently, in the first month of summer, a hunter can usually depend on a few days of seal-hunting to provide more than enough meat to satisfy the immediate needs of his family and his dogs, and enough sealskins to keep his wife busy for weeks thereafter.

In the last week of May, I finally set out with Avataq and his two sons to hunt walrus from the camp at the island's western end. The weather was bad that year, so his wife—a West Greenlander called Marie—decided for the time being to stay at home in the village of Qeqertarssuaq. On reaching the camp, we found that the other wives had made the same decision. Our companions were nine men—hunters and their sons—whose tents were pitched over their sledges on a pebble beach. Their dogs lay tethered nearby; and three motor boats were lined up by the shore. Some 50 yards away, beyond the ice skirting the shoreline, was the open sea, but it was heavily shrouded in mist. We could only imagine the herds of walrus that might be out there, asleep on ice-floes that had carried them south with the current from Smith Sound.

For three full days following our arrival, poor visibility made hunting impossible. The men sat around for hours, brewing tea on their primus stoves, smoking pipes, telling stories, repairing harpoons, cleaning rifles, or carving little animal-like figures from ivory or soap-stone.

In the 24-hour daylight, the men slept when they were tired and ate when they were hungry, without any fixed routine. Always, however, someone remained awake, looking for a sign that the sea-mist was lifting. Then, at last, visibility began to improve and immediately the hunters took to the sea. Three men went out in each motor boat: one at the tiller, two seated with their rifles and harpoons lying beside them.

Walrus-hunting in early summer bears no resemblance whatsoever to the stealthy technique of seeking out walrus on twilight winter treks over bending thin ice. On spotting walrus asleep on an ice-floe, the hunters cut their engines and move in as quietly as possible to within 25 to 50 yards of their prey. But as soon as they come within shooting range, tremendous noise erupts. Rifles fire and engines roar as the hunters race after walrus that have abandoned their ice-floes to seek refuge in the water, or away from angry walrus threatening to strike back. This form of hunting can be as alarming as it is exhilarating. In clear water you can sometimes see a walrus using its massive tail flippers to propel itself directly at your boat, then spinning on to its back in an effort to sink its great tusks into the hull of the craft.

Only a few decades ago, when the Polar Eskimos daringly pursued walrus in kayaks, it was not unusual for a hunter to be drowned or seriously injured.

A Brief Burst of Colour

With the annual summer thaw, the Thule district is transformed for three months from a frigid desert into a fertile tundra. Heaths, bogs and meadows reappear from under thee melting ice, and the ubiquitous white of the winter landscape makes way for the warmer shades of many flowering plants.

The growing season begins in June, when the snow and ice finally retreat and streams bring melt-water down from the permanent ice-sheet to moisten the freshly exposed topsoil below it. Because the 24-hour daylight of the summer months allows photosynthesis to continue round the clock, plants in the Thule district grow unusually quickly.

The species that thrive have to be hardy to survive the rigours of the arctic environment. The sun's warmth rarely penetrates below a depth of about one foot, beneath which the ground is in the grip of a permafrost. The combination of a shallow soil layer and occasional high winds favour small, sturdy plants, few of which grow more than ankle-high.

The flowers, mainly of alpine species, grow in their greatest profusion in the glacial valleys or on hillsides sheltered from the prevailing south-westerly winds. Well-drained slopes come ablaze with purple saxifrage, yellow and white poppies, and the exquisite, bell-shaped flowers of the Lapland cassiope. Clumps of cotton grass, whose heads resemble small clusters of dandelion seeds, line the stream-banks in the valleys.

For the Polar Eskimos, the summer flora has always been a useful resource as well as an aesthetic pleasure. Dried cotton grass has served as a lining for sealskin boots; and the Eskimos used to insert twigs of the arctic willow, topped with tufts of polar bear hair, under their clothes to trap body lice. One traditional practice involving flowers has survived to the present day. Eskimo children still take a special pleasure in chewing the tasty petals of certain species, among them river beauty.

Arctic willow *(Salix arctica)*

River beauty *(Epilobium latifolium)*

Lapland cassiope *(Cassiope tetragona)*

Cotton grass *(Eriophorum)*

Yellow poppy *(Papaver radicatum)*

Lousewort *(Pedicularis lanata)*

Lapland rosebay *(Rhododendron lapponicum)*

Prickly saxifrage *(Saxifraga tricuspidata)*

Chickweed *(Stellaria humifusa)*

Nowadays, these accidents are rare because of the sturdiness and speed of the larger boats; and, of course, the chances of success are greater.

On my first walrus-shoot, I watched two men attack five walrus lying on an ice-floe. They killed two of them outright with rifle shots, and pursued and harpooned another after it had lurched back into the sea. Two escaped.

Back at camp, the men immediately skinned and carved up the three enormous carcasses. Nothing was wasted. The ivory tusks would later be sold for export to the local trading store. One-third of the meat was also set aside for sale, either to the store or to less successful hunters, to provide extra money for buying fuel. The rest of the meat was saved as food for the three hunters' families and for their dogs. The skin, too, was divided up for dog food. The brains were consumed at once, while still warm. So, too, were half-digested clams taken from the walrus' stomachs; these tender morsels are considered great delicacies by the Eskimos.

I have always enjoyed hunting with the Polar Eskimos at their summer camps, but there is one aspect of the camps that has often bemused me: it is impossible to predict their duration. One year, hunters may remain in one place for several weeks; another year they will break camp after a few days and move on elsewhere. The decision is influenced not only by the amount of game in the area. Sometimes the general mood of the camp has as much to do with it. There may be friction between two families, or rivalry between the younger and more headstrong men; or, as often happens, passers-by may bring rumours of exciting hunting elsewhere. The Eskimos love variety, and the thought that they might be missing something can be too much to bear, especially in summer when they strive to live every day to the full.

Such restlessness is especially acute in camps that are populated only by hunters and their sons. There, a zestful spirit of adventure and camaraderie prevails; but there is also a certain competitiveness between the men that brings an element of dare-devilry to the hunt.

By comparison, the atmosphere of the camps made up of entire families is almost sedate. The wives sit outside their tents preparing food, repairing equipment or simply gossiping, while their children play around them. One or two old folk, who have come for the ride and the pleasure of a brief sojourn in the open air, may be outside soaking up the sunlight and reliving memories of their youth over pipes of tobacco or mugs of tea. The atmosphere is festive and communal; often all the families in the camp will gather to eat meals of seal or walrus meat boiled in a single pot. The leisurely approach to hunting in these camps allows more time to appreciate nature, time to drift into tune with a sleepy, sun-drenched polar world and observe the immense richness of its wildlife and scenery.

June is the month when the landscape of the Thule district undergoes its most spectacular change of the year. Thawing on the ice-sheet and on island hills sends great melt-streams roaring down to the sea. The few showers of snow melt almost as soon as the flakes touch the ground. Additional vital moisture is given to the plants by heavy mists drifting in from the sea. Now,

Big Hauls of Little Auks

Arriving in their millions during the last weeks of May, little auks are the most numerous of the migratory sea-birds that flock each summer to the Thule district. These distant cousins of the penguin nest in the high, sun-warmed sea-cliffs of the region which, with their proximity to plankton-rich waters, make ideal breeding grounds. Throughout the summer months, the birds provide the Eskimos with a welcome seasonal supplement to their regular diet.

To make a large catch, hunters and their families will often set up camp beneath the nesting places for several days or weeks. The hunters net little auks on the wing. Although the birds can be hunted throughout the 24 hours of daylight, the best time for catching them is between two and four o'clock in the morning, when they return from their daily feeding trip out to sea and swarm around their nests in locust-like clouds.

Men, women and children all hunt the birds. The only equipment they need is a nylon net set in a wooden hoop at the end of a 10-foot pole. The hunter takes up a partly concealed position in a gully or in a small pit high on the scree slopes below the nesting grounds. When the birds are in the air, the hunter has only to extend his net into their flight-path and sweep the pole towards his prey, twisting it suddenly to secure a catch.

The hunters stuff the carcasses into sacks which are carried down to the camp as they fill up. Many of the birds are then eaten at once, either raw or boiled. The rest are packed into blubber-lined sealskins and left to ferment. The pungent results are regarded by the Eskimos as a great delicacy.

A little auk rests on a rock ledge, its webbed feet tucked beneath its plump body, about eight inches long. After wintering farther south, the birds return to the Thule district to nest year after year on the same cliffs.

At the foot of a cliff where little auks nest, hunters and their families busy themselves around tents pitched on moss-covered rock.

Seated on a scree slope, a hunter nets a victim from a fluttering cloud of little auks. Once the bird is trapped, the hunter hauls in the pole hand over hand and disentangles his prey from the netting. He kills the bird instantaneously by pressing his thumb on its heart to stop the blood-flow, then adds the carcass to the pile already collected in the sack at his feet.

Back at the camp, the hunter empties the contents of his sack on to the rest of the day's catch. In the course of a four or five-day stay in a camp, one hunter can expect to catch at least a thousand birds, which will be used to feed his family as well as his dogs, and perhaps a few visiting friends or relatives.

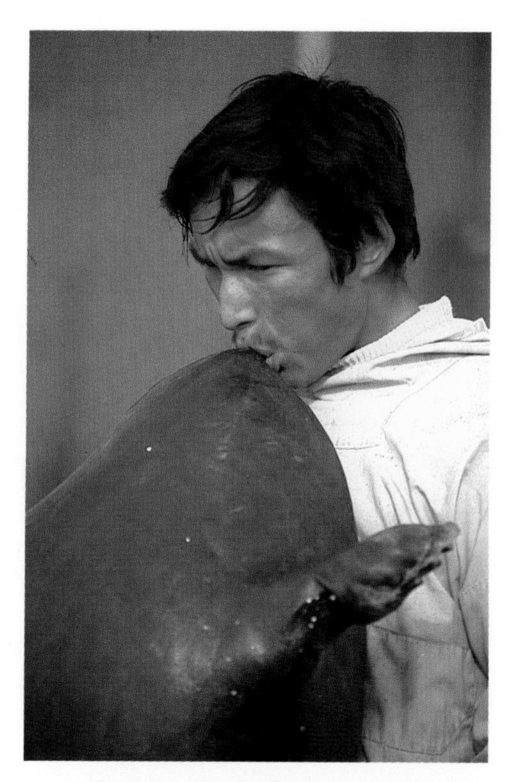

In preparation for the open-water hunting season, a Polar Eskimo inflates a float made from a sealskin complete with fore-flippers. A small mouthpiece in the neck opening, fitted with a wooden plug, allows the float to be blown up or deflated. Attached to a harpoon line, the float serves as a drag to tire sea prey when they dive and as a marker when they rise again to the water's surface.

all at once, one discovers that, stripped of its white shroud, the land is very much alive—with vegetation, with insects, and especially with birds.

It is an amazing time of birth and of renewal. After wintering beneath the frozen surface in larval or egg form, flies, mosquitoes, bumblebees, spiders, beetles, mites and multi-coloured butterflies emerge into the light of day. Now, too, plants come out of long hibernation to recommence their growth and store sufficient nourishment to survive another nine or 10 months of dormancy. Their time for vegetation is brief; plants cannot grow in sub-zero temperatures, and in most years in the Thule district the mean temperature is above freezing-point for only three months—from late May to late August. But nature compensates for the shortness of the season by way of 24-hour sunlight that allows photosynthesis to continue uninterrupted throughout this transitory, life-giving span.

Above all, it is the enormous influx of migratory birds that enriches this awakening world. In the winter months, the only birds to be seen are that hardy trio: the raven, snowy owl and ptarmigan. Bird-calls are rare; and outside the villages, the arctic landscape is sometimes as silent as a soundproof chamber. The return of the migrating birds in May brings welcome relief to the impoverished ear; but it is in June—the egg-laying month for the majority of species—that a glorious cacophony of bird-song fills the air around each stretch of open water and every sea-cliff suitable for nesting.

The variety of birds is truly fascinating to behold: wide-winged, high-soaring glaucous gulls robbing nests and scavenging on the discarded remains of seals killed by polar bears; eider-ducks stepping out of their down-lined nests and leading newly hatched chicks into open water; snow geese, now so rare as to be a protected species; kittiwakes carrying back small fish to their chicks nesting on narrow cliff ledges; heavily billed fulmars gracefully gliding over the sea and bobbing for food; regal, fast-flying gyrfalcons sweeping through the sky in pursuit of ptarmigan; and arctic terns, fantastic long-range fliers that have been known to cover more than 25,000 miles a year.

No bird, however, is found in greater number than the dovekie, or little auk. Every summer this smallest of migratory sea-birds is slaughtered on a huge scale by the Polar Eskimos. Congregating by the million in tenement cliff colonies, they are so prolific that their population is beyond estimation. Their numbers never visibly diminish.

My first encounter with little auks in massed flight came about one day in early June when Avataq and I were returning to our camp on Herbert Island from a hunting trip to the far western end of Northumberland Island. We were travelling at no more than one knot, because lashed to the sides of Avataq's small motor-powered boat were the carcasses of three bull walrus. But we did not care about speed. It was about 2 a.m. on a beautiful, clear morning with the sea absolutely calm and gleaming like a mirror in the bright sunlight. Except for the gentle chugging of the outboard motor, all was silence. We felt completely at peace with the world.

Then, suddenly, we became aware of a distant whirring sound that second by second became louder until soon a veritable thunder of beating wings filled the air. Flying directly across our course were hundreds of thousands of little auks. The birds were flocked in a swirling, scudding cloud that briefly blotted out the sun. Avataq explained that they were flying towards the bird cliffs of Siorapaluk after a spell of feeding at sea. He went on to describe the vast colony of little auks breeding in holes in the cliffs and the holiday atmosphere of the hunters' camp below them where families gather to net and kill the birds. He also told me that the sound of the birds was "like nothing on earth—as though the cliffs themselves were alive".

In addition to the cliffs at Siorapaluk—an especially popular hunting ground, because it is close by a permanent settlement—there are several other areas in the Thule district where, every summer from May to late August, tens of thousands of birds are killed to provide a welcome supplement to the Polar Eskimos' diet.

Sometimes the birds are simply plucked and eaten raw, still warm from life. More often, however, they are cooked—complete with their feathers, to avoid the tedious chore of plucking—in boiling, salted water for 20 minutes or so. As they cook, the outer layer of fat seeps into the flesh to make the bird more succulent. After boiling, the birds are promptly rubbed in snow to cool them. The wings are broken off, then the skin and feathers can be stripped off in one movement by pinching the skin at the back of the bird's neck and pulling gently. It is as easy as pulling off a sock. The Eskimos eat the rest of the bird, including the fat; they only spit out the bones.

Little auks are also used to make the most elaborate and exotic of all Polar Eskimo dishes: *kiviaq*. To prepare this delicacy, literally hundreds of birds are bound up in a complete sealskin for six months or more; the putrefying end-product is then eaten raw.

The first steps in making *kiviaq* are to net the birds, and to hunt and kill a seal. The seal's innards then have to be cut out and removed through the mouth to leave the skin and its adjoining layer of blubber intact. After this operation, you have in effect an enormous, blubber-lined sealskin sack. It is then filled to the brim with little auks complete with feathers, bills, legs and claws. When it becomes impossible to press in even one more bird, the sealskin sack is sewn up—traditionally with narwhal sinew, though now more often with dental floss—and placed in a cairn of rocks. No direct sunlight should penetrate this cairn. If all goes well and the cairn is not raided by foxes, by Christmas the contents of the sack should be ready to eat.

By this time the birds have usually reached an advanced stage of decomposition and the seal blubber has penetrated deep into their flesh, so adding to the unique flavour of the *kiviaq*. That flavour—something like oily, overripe Camembert—is certainly not to my taste, but most Polar Eskimos regard it as a great treat. They consume the dish raw, simply picking out inedible feathers, beaks and bones with their fingers as they eat. No dish is greeted with greater delight at weddings and confirmation celebrations.

In late summer, narwhal is the hunters' prime quarry. Earlier in the season, isolated narwhal are from time to time killed in open water by hunters in boats. But it is only in late July and August, when whole schools come into the fiords, that this form of hunting comes to supersede all others.

The most popular hunting grounds for narwhal are at the eastern, inland end of Inglefield Sound, around the village at Qeqertat. But ever since my two-year stay in Qeqertarssuaq, my own favourite base for narwhal-hunting has been a camp at the eastern tip of Herbert Island, near the Sound's mouth. At first glance, it is a hostile-looking place; the coastline there is rugged, and always, towering above, is the sharp crest of the island, a central hill that stands out like a great black dragon when its slopes are in shadow. But this corner of the island also has many small sequestered spots cushioned with spongy grass and cut with tiny streams. Here, most especially, the Eskimos' love of summer is reflected in their relaxed and happy mood.

It was at this camp that the veteran hunter, Taitsianguaratsiaq, once called me aside secretly and beckoned me to follow him up a nearby scree slope. We scrambled about 300 yards over some formidable boulders and rock falls; then, following the course of a little stream, we climbed towards one enormous rock that hovered above us. "I will show you my grandmother's cave," said Taitsianguaratsiaq.

After many long rests to catch his breath, Taitsianguaratsiaq, then in his sixties, led me to the huge boulder that dominated all others on the rocky slope. "There!" he said, pointing to the rock. "Can you see it? That is where my grandmother made her cave."

There was nothing to see except a tiny niche in the rock face: virtually a dent, no more than three feet high and two feet deep. The old hunter continued, "She made it herself. Cut it out with a stone that was harder than the rock." He pointed to scratches on the wall and with an outstretched arm traced the outline of the hole. "See the shape!" he urged. "See the shape!"

Then he curled himself into a foetal position on a grassy bank nearby to show me exactly how his grandmother had moulded herself into the rock; and now, as I looked closely at the hole, I could almost see her in there and feel her presence. I was about to say so when my old friend suddenly broke into a traditional Polar Eskimo chant—an ululating song without words that represented a tribute to the past and his hopes for the future. There were tears in his eyes when he finished.

I was silent. I wanted to ask Taitsianguaratsiaq why she had made the "cave" but he was so moved that the question stuck in my throat. In any case, I found out the answer later that night, when an east wind devastated our camp, blowing away four tents and scaring us half to death. We wrapped ourselves in whatever blankets and clothing we could salvage and pressed ourselves against the rocks to avoid the full blast of the icy gale. And then I saw the need for the old woman's exertions. The niche she had made was her shelter from the wind; no one else could use it because it had been designed to fit her alone. It still belonged to her in spirit.

That storm in late July brought the first gale-force winds of summer. They blew for two full days and smashed up the last of the sea-ice that blocked the fiords, opening the way for schools of narwhal to penetrate the inner reaches

Riding the calm waters of a fiord, a kayak-borne hunter launches a harpoon with the aid of a throwing stick. Initially laid flat between the two white hooks on the harpoon's shaft, the throwing stick pivots from the rear hook as the harpoon is released, lengthening the arc of the hunter's throw and so imparting extra velocity. The weapon is attached by a 60-foot-long rope to a sealskin float behind the hunter.

of Inglefield Sound, due east of Herbert Island. In so doing, they also gave the hunters in our camp access to the sea and the chance to pursue the whales.

I set out with Avataq and his sons in a motor boat as soon as the storm had abated. Because a local conservation measure forbids the use of such boats to hunt whales in the Sound during high season, we also took kayaks aboard. The weather was balmy once more and on a sea like glass we moved slowly along the southern shore of the fiord. Silencing the engine, we then rowed out from the coast and there we waited for 15 hours—drifting, soaking up the sun, smoking pipes and talking to each other in whispers so as not to frighten away any incoming narwhal. The sparkle given off the water was blinding, the tranquillity almost unearthly.

Then, at last, a few hundred yards away to our stern, we saw the first school of narwhal passing by. Their presence indicated that other schools would soon follow. Immediately, Avataq and I lowered our kayaks into the sea and set off in the direction that the whales had taken, leaving the larger boat in the care of Avataq's sons.

Avataq, leading the way, paddled for about 200 yards, then turned his kayak at right angles to the direction the narwhal had taken. I headed in the same direction and lined up parallel with him, some 30 yards away. We were now well positioned, with a wide field of view to our front and right—the direction from which the whales would come.

For a full hour we sat still and silent in our kayaks, the sea mirroring us like figures in a single frame of film as we waited with nothing else to do but meditate, feel the sensual warmth of the sun, and all the while scan the waters for signs of whales. Then they came—about 20 of them, their curved, brown-speckled white backs breaking the surface so slowly that they caused barely a ripple. They came so close that I could have reached out with my paddle to touch them and I could almost smell their steamy breath as they exhaled with a soft blowing sound.

For two, perhaps three, minutes the narwhal passed within harpoon range. I could not understand why Avataq did not make a move. Then, at last, he took up his paddle, gently turned his kayak and began to follow the whales. Watching him steadily increase his pace and rhythmically slice the surface of the water with a minimum of noise, I realized that he had bided his time until the narwhal were ahead of him so that he could stalk them from behind.

After covering about 50 yards, Avataq stopped paddling, transferred his paddle to his left hand and reached for his harpoon: a six-foot wooden shaft with a detachable head of ivory. It was lying on the kayak deck on his right-hand side. Behind it, neatly coiled, was a nylon line, some 60 feet long, that was attached at one end to the harpoon head. The line itself was linked at one point to a square wooden frame covered with sealskin that was designed to act as a drag when it hit the water. Finally, the other end was attached to an inflated sealskin that would serve both as a marker buoy and as an additional drag if Avataq sank the harpoon into a narwhal.

Avataq held his weapon aloft for seconds that seemed like minutes. Then he threw it, aiming at a narwhal that had surfaced only 10 to 15 feet from his kayak. Almost simultaneously, he pushed the sealskin float with the drag-frame over the side and took a two-handed grip on his paddle. But there was no time to get out of the way. He had barely taken a stroke before the narwhal dived, its tail flipper making an almighty splash that rocked the kayak alarmingly. In fact, Avataq had timed his strike to perfection. He was just close enough for his harpoon to carry through the whale's skin, but not so close that the narwhal's thrashing tail would capsize his frail craft.

Now all was quiet again and we could only wait. Sometimes a harpooned narwhal will sound for as long as 20 minutes, during which time the hunter's patience is tested to the utmost by a tense and harrowing vigil. But on this occasion, we were lucky. Perhaps two minutes elapsed before the sealskin float bobbed to the surface. Then Avataq and I paddled furiously towards the marker so as to be within reasonably close range when the whale came up for air. It surfaced shortly afterwards—only 30 yards away, heaving and throbbing in a blood-red sea.

Traditionally, after an initial strike with a harpoon, hunters struggled to finish off a narwhal by spearing it with lances. A few Polar Eskimos still kill the whales in this way, but most hunters now use rifles to dispatch their quarry quickly and efficiently.

On this occasion, Avataq used a .303 rifle. One shot was enough at such close range. It remained for us to haul in the narwhal with the harpoon line, attach additional sealskin floats to the carcass for buoyancy and lash it to one side of our supporting boat.

I have seen similar harpoon feats by other great hunters, but I will remember this one most vividly of all because of the magical setting and the blissful hours of waiting on a silent fiord where every image had its double in the mirror of a tranquil sea. On such a day, the human predator seems to be an integral part of the natural world around him. This, in essence, is what always attracts me to the world of the Polar Eskimos, where the arctic environment, harsh though it may be, has dictated the way of life for hundreds of years.

In Search of the Sea Unicorn

In July each year, as the sea-ice breaks up, Eskimos from all over the Thule district, accompanied by their families, head for 55-mile-long Inglefield Sound to hunt narwhal: small arctic whales up to 18 feet long that migrate in their hundreds each summer from Baffin Bay to the inlet, where they calve and feed on the seasonal shoals of fish and cuttlefish.

Known to sailors in the past as the sea unicorn because of the male's long tusk, the narwhal was heavily exploited by whalers in the 19th century. In recent times, it has been pursued chiefly by the Eskimos of the Greenland and Canadian coasts, for whom it offers a rich prize of ivory, meat, oil and hide. Because of over-hunting, however, its numbers are in decline. As a result, in a local conservation measure, all narwhal now killed in Thule district waters must first be harpooned—a move that is designed to prevent excessive slaughter by hunters armed only with rifles and to limit kills to the present average of about 100 a year.

The families camp out in tents at any one of a number of sites from which whales have been pursued for centuries past. There they take turns keeping watch for the approaching schools of narwhal throughout the hours of daylight. If the weather remains calm, delaying the final dispersal of the ice, they may wait weeks for a sighting.

Once the quarry finally appears, the hunters race to board their kayaks, which are painted white as camouflage against the background of small icebergs and floes. Their aim is to approach close enough to hurl their harpoons at their prey. Attached to each harpoon line are a sealskin float and drag anchor that tire the injured whale as it dives repeatedly to escape its assailants. When the whale finally becomes exhausted—sometimes as much as an hour after the chase began—the hunters deliver the *coup de grâce* by shooting it with a rifle or else by puncturing its lungs with lances.

From a high vantage point, a hunter scans the sea for narwhal with binoculars. His bedding is in a rocky niche below, where he rests between watches.

Holding the throwing stick used to hurl a lance with great force, a hunter dispatches a surfacing narwhal (inset, above). The whale, already weakened by two harpoons attached by lines to sealskin floats, thrashes the blood-stained sea with its tail as it struggles in its death throes (right).

Towed ashore after the kill, a bull narwhal lies beached (inset, right) while the hunters wait for the tide to recede and give them a firm footing on which to carve up their quarry. The head and tail are removed first (below) so that the trunk can be rolled over easily. The hide—a source of vitamins that is eaten raw as a delicacy—is stripped off and divided, with the meat, among the hunters.

Jakob Petersen, the first hunter to anchor his harpoon in the narwhal, stands proudly holding its seven-foot-long tusk, which will fetch a high price for him at the local trading store. "Jako, you'll be a millionaire," his friends teased. The tusks are exported for sale as rare and valuable curios.

A hunter washes his share of the intestines in the waters of an inlet already turned blood-red by the butchering of the bull narwhal on the shoreline.

Five | Building a Future on the Past

Over the years, I had become a close friend of old Taitsianguaratsiaq, the father of my hunting companion Avataq. Well past 70 at the time of my last visit, Taitsianguaratsiaq remained healthy and energetic, and I was delighted to find that he still ran a dog team of his own, although he was long beyond the age at which most Polar Eskimos give up hunting. The challenge of the hunt was to him the very stuff of life; he embraced the hardships and suffering that it entailed. Yet, Taitsianguaratsiaq did not admire hardship for its own sake and was grateful for many of the comforts that recent decades had brought the Polar Eskimos. Listening to his stories of the past, I came to appreciate just how grim their existence had once been.

The most tragic story Taitsianguaratsiaq ever told me was an episode not from his own life but from that of his father Qaerngaq. As a young man, Qaerngaq had been wintering in the far north of the Thule district with his own father Qumangapik and 13 other relatives. Hunting was very poor and, by February, the coldest part of the year, the reserves of meat and blubber were gone. Faced with starvation, the group headed south in search of game or the help of other Eskimos.

The party set off by sledge down the coast. They had travelled most of the way to the nearest settlement when they were overtaken by a blizzard. On Qumangapik's orders, they at once set about building igloos that would shelter them until the weather improved. Later, no one could remember exactly how long the storm raged. In any case, because there was no blubber to serve as fuel for their lamps, which normally provide both warmth and light, the igloos did not provide sufficient protection against the elements. By the time the winds finally abated some days later, Qumangapik and 10 other members of the party were dead.

The four survivors were reduced to killing and eating their dogs to ward off starvation. When all the dogs were dead, they faced up to the fact that their only hope of salvation lay in using the last of their strength to push onwards

to the nearest known shelter. Even so, one man was already too weak to travel and they had to leave him behind, with a meagre stock of dog meat, to meet his fate; eventually he was found dead in his igloo. Qaerngaq himself pushed a sledge carrying the other two survivors over the last few miles to their destination: the haven of a relative's hut. An eyewitness to the arrival of the three exhausted, frost-bitten travellers later recalled seeing Qaerngaq cut off his own gangrenous little toe.

The story is far from unique in the history of the Polar Eskimos. Indeed, Qumangapik himself, in his youth, had brushed closely with death during the attempt led by the great shaman Qitdlarssuaq to return from the Thule district to his native village in Canada. Qitdlarssuaq, by then an old man, died of exhaustion early in the trek; the rest of the 15-strong party tried to continue without him, but during the second winter of the journey ran out of food completely and some members of the group resorted to cannibalism. The bodies of Qumangapik's own parents, both of whom had starved to death, were consumed by their fellows and it was only Qumangapik's intervention that saved his brother, who was still alive though weakened, from being murdered and suffering a similar fate. As as result of the attack on his brother, Qumangapik decided to turn back towards Thule, taking his brother and their two families with him. He finally reached the district five years after setting out. By that time, not only his parents, but also his wife and one of his three children, had died of hunger or exposure. The dreadful hardships he suffered were not typical, since few Polar Eskimos had ever attempted such extended journeys; but in those days all knew what it was like to suffer and go without food.

Now, the spoils of hunting are supplemented by an abundance of imported foodstuffs, brought to the town of Qânâq each summer by supply ships from Denmark and distributed among the trading stores situated in each of the villages. In the shops, provisions are available—on credit, if necessary—

to hungry families. Even in winter, when the sea route to the district is blocked by ice, vital supplies can be flown in by air via the Thule Air Base.

Medical attention, too, is relatively easy to come by. At least one resident in every settlement is trained in first aid and supplied with a wide range of pharmaceuticals stored in numbered bottles. In cases of straightforward illness, this part-time paramedic can radio the hospital in Qânâq, describe the patient's symptoms and receive in answer a prescription by numbers. In extreme emergency, a doctor can be summoned to the village either by dog sledge or by helicopter from the air base—provided, of course, that weather conditions permit travelling.

The value of medical aid—most notably in eradicating tuberculosis and cutting the infant mortality rate by nearly two-thirds—is clearly reflected in the district's census figures. In the 19th and early 20th centuries, there was an average of four children to each family, yet the Polar Eskimo population remained fairly stable at between 200 and 250. By the beginning of the 1980s, the population had reached 750 and was still rising, despite the introduction of family-planning measures that cut the birth-rate by more than half. The explorer Commander Robert Peary once observed that Polar Eskimos very rarely lived for more than 60 years; now the Thule district usually has at least a score of septuagenarians—and even a few octogenarians. Some of the Eskimos are prone to bronchial ailments caused by exposure to cold and wind, and often aggravated by heavy smoking. But contagious diseases are rare because most harmful viruses are rendered inactive by the cold; and, curiously, diabetes is unknown—much to the interest of medical researchers.

These social advances are counterbalanced by other, less happy influences brought in from the West. The most blatantly damaging importation is drunkenness—an evil first introduced to the Thule region by the whalers in the 19th century who artfully plied the Eskimos with spirits before bargaining with them for skins and furs. In the 1960s, when regular supplies of alcoholic beverages were first shipped in to meet the demand from Danish administrators and technicians, drunkenness was so rampant that the local authorities introduced rationing on a points system. A bottle of beer represented one point, a bottle of spirits counted for 20. Every adult in the district, whether Danish or Eskimo, was allowed a monthly ration of 30 points.

The system, however, was largely ineffective in curbing excesses, since the Eskimos tended to consume their entire monthly ration in one riotous drinking session. Therefore, in 1976, a weekly 10-point ration was allocated. It reduced the amount of alcohol available at any one time, but the habit of concentrated drinking was not broken.

Another disruptive force—and a common complaint raised by the older Eskimos—is the growing acquisitiveness of the younger generation. At the beginning of this century, the Polar Eskimos spent the winters in tiny one-room houses made of stone and insulated by banks of turf set around the walls. These dwellings had no surplus space for storing possessions; they were, simply, shelters in which to eat and sleep. Every two or three years, when the houses had become unpleasantly dirty and fetid, the families

During a halt on a hunting trip, an Eskimo uses a saw to cut frozen polar bear meat for boiling, while a companion brews tea on a primus stove. Such Western artefacts are now standard equipment for sledge-drivers, mitigating the hardships of arctic travel.

abandoned them and moved into new homes, often in a different settlement. In those days, no one owned more goods than he could carry on a sledge. Now that each family has a permanent home, however, there is the opportunity to accumulate possessions. The range of goods available to the Eskimos has also increased as the flow of imports from Denmark has swelled.

To pay for these imports, the Eskimos require cash, which they receive from the trading stores in return for the skins and furs of the animals they kill. A monetary economy has replaced the old methods of bartering goods by exchange. The Eskimos can even borrow money on generous terms from the government to pay for major acquisitions, such as the motor boats they use in the summer months when the sea-ice recedes. And they also have government-financed mortgages to help them buy the modern houses now being constructed in all the villages of the district.

These material changes have inevitably affected the Polar Eskimos' view of life. Although the vast majority covet the new comforts, few Eskimos would deny that easy contact with the outside world has inflicted a deep-seated malaise on their society. One of its most disturbing symptoms is the increasing incidence of suicide. Most villages have experienced at least one tragedy of this kind within the recent past, and the victims have included some of the district's finest hunters. Their deaths remain largely unexplained and without any evident motive. Yet it seems likely that they spring from a terrible form of identity crisis, a fatal loss of self-esteem ensuing from the clash of two very different cultures.

At a village school, a pupil carves a notch for extra lashing in a crosspiece of a child's sledge. Under the instruction of an old hunter, boys learn not only how to make sledges but also how to hammer out metal harpoon heads and stitch dog harnesses.

By a strange irony, the growing links with the outside world that have caused the Polar Eskimos such problems have also offered them, for the first time in their history, a degree of choice about how to live their lives. In the past, there was no alternative to their harsh, traditional lifestyle; they had to hunt in order to survive. Now, however, some of the younger Eskimos, at least, have options. Women can aspire to jobs as teachers, secretaries, nurses or shop assistants. Alternatively, they may hope to escape the confinement of the life of a hunter's wife by marrying one of the Danish technicians working in Qânâq. For men, there occasionally are jobs within the district with the Royal Greenland Trade Department, as clerks, storekeepers or odd-job men, and with the Greenland Technical Organization, as carpenters, builders or mechanics. Admittedly, much of the work is menial and there are relatively few local openings. But it is also now not unusual for young Polar Eskimos to go to southern Greenland or Denmark to complete their education. Furthermore, there is no legal barrier to prevent them from staying on after their schooling is finished to seek a comfortable livelihood in their new location.

Few do, however. Of those who leave the district in search of an alternative lifestyle, more than half return. Sometimes they come back because of home-sickness, sometimes because of difficulties in finding acceptable work. When they do come back, they tend to see the district and its people in a fresh perspective. Often they bring with them a commitment to the wave of nationalism that has swept through the entire Eskimo race in recent years. The whole community, in fact, now shares a heightened sense of cultural identity with other Eskimo groups overseas. Like their cousins in Canada and Alaska, the Polar Eskimos refer to themselves as "Inuit"—the Eskimo word meaning "real men", which in the Polar Eskimo dialect is pronounced as "Inussuit", a usage unique to the Thule district. Encouragingly, they also tend to display a new sense of pride in their native land.

On my last trip to the Arctic, I met one young man who in my view personified the dilemma of the young, educated Polar Eskimo. In the most literal sense, he was a product of the two cultures: he was the grandson of an illegitimate son of Commander Peary. Sometimes he called himself Robert Edwin Peary, though more often he used his given name: Sigssuk. Both of his parents were politically active in Qânâq. Indeed his father, a respected hunter, had been the district's elected representative in the Greenland legislature in Godthaab, the country's capital, a thousand miles to the south.

In his late teens, Sigssuk had been sent to college in Copenhagen to complete a course of general studies especially designed for Greenlanders. Like so many of the youngsters who leave the Thule district, however, he soon came to feel trapped between two different ways of life. He was cut off from his roots and felt at a disadvantage in his contacts with young Danes—people of an alien cultural heritage. He was very unhappy and decided to go home.

After returning to Qânâq, Sigssuk took a job at the Thule Air Base. In a sense, he was lucky to get it: to minimize its intrusion into the Polar Eskimos' lives, the air base usually followed a policy of employing only Danes. But he still felt trapped. He was given work as a laundry-hand, then as a janitor. Such occupations deeply offended his innate and powerful intelligence, and demanded the one thing he could not supply: his undivided application for eight boring hours of every work day six days a week. Also, Sigssuk did not subscribe to the work ethic of his employers, nor their concept of regular time-keeping. Neither did he feel comfortable in a subservient role.

Sigssuk had an uncle and a brother who had failed to come to terms with their fast-changing world and had committed suicide. Gradually, he came to see their deaths as a terrible warning to his people. The moral that he drew from the experience was that only by committing themselves to traditional values could the younger generation of Polar Eskimos save themselves from a continuing decline and, ultimately, ethnic extinction. Finally, he came to a momentous decision; in pursuit of a more meaningful existence, he took up the traditional life of a hunter.

Eager, tense, articulate and passionately proud of his race, Sigssuk was also relatively prosperous after three years on the air-base payroll. He loved modern gadgetry and had even bought himself a snowmobile—still a rarity in the Thule district. But when I left him, he was driving only a dog sledge, and talking enthusiastically and idealistically about his plans to get back to the true Eskimo life: to support himself by hunting and to travel far north with other hunters in search of polar bear.

Only time will tell whether he will succeed in his ambitions. Idealism on its own cannot make a hunter, and it will take years of hard work for Sigssuk to learn the harsh realities of the way of life to which he aspires. Nevertheless,

An Eskimo woman softens a sealskin sole for a new pair of boots by chewing it. Without some such preparation, the thick, bearded sealskin used for boot soles is too tough to sew. Many women hammer the skin with a stone, but chewing is the superior method: it damages the skin less, leaving the boot sole more waterproof and hard-wearing.

his quest for identity is indicative of a new awakening of ethnic pride among the Polar Eskimos. The younger, educated hunters increasingly measure the decades of well-meant Danish influence in terms of losses as well as gains and recognize the need to safeguard their cultural inheritance.

The Polar Eskimo way of life has always been inextricably bound up with hunting, so it is hardly surprising that the traditional culture of the Thule district is more alive in the smaller settlements, where most of the hunters live, than in Qânâq. In the outlying villages, parents are still passing on the old skills and values to the coming generation. The process can begin literally in the cradle, which some hunter fathers make in the shape of a kayak. Suspended in his kayak-rocker from a beam in the ceiling, a male infant soon learns to keep a steady keel by stroking the air with a toy paddle. Every now and then a passing adult will gently rock the tiny kayak and judge how well the child is able to maintain his balance in the craft—a vital skill for later life, since most Polar Eskimo hunters, living three-quarters of the year in sub-zero temperatures, never learn to swim.

As soon as he can walk, a hunter's son will be given a husky puppy, together with a miniature harness and a toy whip, so that he becomes accustomed early in life to handling and disciplining dogs. Girls, too, learn how to handle a whip to impose their authority on dog teams. But the principal lesson girls learn from their mothers is how to clean sealskins and make fur clothes, in preparation for the chores that will occupy much of their adult lives.

In each village primary school, and in the secondary school at Qânâq, some hunting instruction is given, sometimes by hunters too old to earn their living any longer on the ice. Typically, there will be craft classes for the youths, including demonstrations of how to build kayaks and shape metal harpoon heads; for the girls, there are lessons in preparing and sewing animal skins. But these efforts to adapt the syllabus to local customs are not much more than token gestures; by far the greater part of any child's practical education in the traditional Polar Eskimo skills comes from the parents.

From the age of eight onwards, a boy will often accompany his father on hunting trips. At first he will help with the easier and less risky tasks: laying seal nets, or helping to retrieve the carcasses of game that father has killed. He will learn how to paddle a kayak under an adult's supervision, and will acquire driving skills by hitching two or three dogs from his father's team to a small sledge he may have made himself in school. By the time he reaches his teens, he will be expected to have mastered all the essential skills, and will be waiting restlessly for the day when, at the age of 16 or 17, his father will invite him for the first time to accompany him on a bear hunt. Throughout his education, his father will be an eager, though sometimes impatient, mentor. Indeed, when a boy returns home from the school in Qânâq, he is likely to be told: "Now you can start learning something useful."

So, the techniques of the Eskimo hunter's craft are being passed on to each new generation just as they always have been in the past. But the survival of

Sitting astride a toboggan hitched to a pair of huskies from his father's pack, a hunter's son practises the technique of sledge-driving. By the time they have reached their teens, most Polar Eskimo boys can control a full-sized team of 12 to 15 dogs.

the traditional way of life in the Thule district depends quite as much on the continuing presence of animals to hunt; and here, too, there are hopeful signs for the future. Since 1900, a steady improvement in the climate has led to a marked increase in the number of seals, foxes and little auks in the region, and consequently to a surer supply of prey. In addition, the Eskimos have become increasingly conscious of the need for wildlife conservation. This awareness, fostered by the Danish educationalists and administrators who work with the Eskimos, has further reduced the risks of a shortage of game.

Self-imposed restrictions on the use of the rifle, as opposed to the harpoon, now ensure that the Eskimos do not overhunt walrus and narwhal. Polar bears are protected by a ban on killing bears that are in cub. Fox-trapping is similarly prohibited in the summer breeding-period. Also, caribou—hunted to extinction in the district during the 19th century—have been reintroduced from southern Greenland to the northern shore of Olrik Fiord.

Admittedly, it has not been so easy to make the Polar Eskimos protective towards bird-life. In summer, when an abundance of migratory species flock to the district, hunters are naturally inclined to treat anything on the wing as fair game. Moreover, many children love to lay snares—circles of wire or string designed to trap birds by their legs. In this pursuit they are encouraged by their parents, who like to see them developing their hunting skills.

When a child comes home proudly bearing a snared arctic tern, he is immediately praised. "You will be a great hunter like your father one day," his mother will tell him. Like her husband, she looks forward eagerly to the next sign of his developing prowess—the day when he will snare his first fulmar or perhaps bring home the egg of a rare snow goose.

Even while the parents are encouraging the young hunter, his grandfather may be talking nostalgically about the abundance of bird-life when he was a boy, when there were a great many nesting geese near the village and the eggs—so good to eat—were easy to collect. And the parents will sagely agree with him, seeing little or no connection between the disappearance of the geese and the ravaging of their nests.

Yet, the Polar Eskimos are nothing if not practical in their outlook. Whenever they can see that conservation measures are to their material advantage, they will attempt to respect them. Thus, they accept that only for two days in June each year may they collect the eggs of the eider-duck—a restriction that allows the birds to lay a second clutch. As a result, the eider-ducks, which were once slaughtered almost to extinction, have now re-established themselves in vast colonies on the islands off the district's coast, and the Eskimos have a rich new source of food.

This is progress in the true sense of the word. So long as the fine ecological balance among the arctic species is maintained, the Eskimos will have the raw materials necessary to sustain their traditional way of life. The question then is reduced to one of motivation: the hunting lifestyle can survive only as long as there are men who want to hunt.

In my view, the future of the Polar Eskimos lies not so much with their educated activists and idealists, important though they may be, as with those

Accompanying himself on a sealskin tambour, whose wooden frame he beats with an antler drumstick, an old hunter sings a drum-song. Characterized by lengthy, repetitive refrains, these improvised chants about hunting and other themes from everyday life constitute the only musical tradition of the Polar Eskimos.

After four months of winter darkness, the returning sun bathes the polar landscape in a brief, suffused glow. In just 12 minutes' time it will set once more, dipping out of sight behind the iceberg on the horizon.

young men who spend their formative years serving their apprenticeship as hunters, the time-honoured vocation of their people.

I see Itukusuk as a model for these young men. Educated at the boarding-school in Qânâq, he is perfectly literate, though in practice he has little time for reading and rarely does more than glance through his son's comic books. What he would consider his real education came during years of hunting trips at his father's side. Now his lifestyle is typical of that of the skilled and successful latter-day hunter. He is always eager to be where the game is; he soon becomes restless if compelled by bad weather to stay at home for several days. After a successful hunt, however, he will happily sleep for a whole day to restore his energy before setting out once more in pursuit of game. Indeed, I once knew him to remain in bed for three days on end while high winds made hunting impossible. When teased about this, he merely grinned and replied, "The wind carries sleep."

The seasons continue to affect his life profoundly, just as they have shaped the lives of all Polar Eskimo hunters in the past. The winter months are the time for single-day sorties after seal at sites close to his Moriussaq home. The trips lengthen with the return of the sun. In March, he invariably sets out with other hunters on a longer trek in search of polar bear. When the summer thaw gets under way, he generally leaves Moriussaq at the earliest opportunity to go in search of open water; there from his 14-foot motor boat he hunts seal and walrus at the ice-edge. Unlike most Polar Eskimo hunters, Itukusuk is wealthy enough to own a second, larger boat: a fishing smack that he keeps moored in Qânâq throughout most of the year. In the late summer, he uses this vessel to carry him back and forth down Inglefield Sound to Qeqertat, where he hunts narwhal.

By his assiduity and talent, he has over the years amassed other signs of material success. He owns a dog team more than 20 strong, and his huskies are among the best fed and trained in the Thule district. He and his wife Sofie keep open house for their many relatives and friends, and entertain all comers generously. Itukusuk's wardrobe is always in good condition and he makes sure that he has a new pair of polar bear pants to wear each year.

His attitude towards his profession is pragmatic. I once heard him describing his way of life to adolescents who hoped to follow in his footsteps. "It is all a matter of hard work," he said. "The great hunters are those who go out in all weathers to bring back the meat while the dreamers are still sleeping."

The driving force that spurs on Itukusuk and his kind is, I believe, a phenomenon as old and as powerful as life itself: the need to take part in the ritual game of life and death through which man seeks and finds an affinity with his environment. Indeed, the hunter might claim in one of his rare philosophical moods that this act is man's most venerable pursuit, and that the bond that exists between hunter and hunted is the hunter's proof that he is a man.

The urge that the hunter feels to prove himself as the master-predator in a savage world is as old as the Eskimo race itself. And for as long as that need remains a passion, the Polar Eskimo hunters will continue to live in the style of their ancestors, driving their dog teams over the sea-ice in the darkness of winter, stalking in their kayaks in the bright summer sunlight, and all the while in their hearts reasserting their manly superiority over the thousands of millions of people who live in the easier world to their south.

Bibliography

Alexander, B. and C., *Eskimo Boy*. Adam & Charles Black, London, 1979.

Armstrong, T., Roberts, B., and Swithinbank, C., *Illustrated Glossary of Snow and Ice*. The Scott Polar Research Institute, Cambridge, 1973. Special Publication.

Baird, P.D., *The Polar World*. Longmans, Green & Co., London, 1964.

Banks, Michael, *Greenland*. David & Charles, Newton Abbot, Devon, 1975.

Birket-Smith, Kaj, *The Eskimos*. Translated by W.E. Calvert. Revised translation by Professor C. Daryll Forde. Methuen & Co., London, 1936. Revised edition 1959.

Ekblaw, W.E., *Eskimo Dogs – Forgotten Heroes*. Natural History, vol. 37, New York, 1936.

Ekblaw, W.E., *The Material Response of the Polar Eskimo to their Far Arctic Environment*. Annals of the Association of American Geographers, vol. 17 (4), Chicago, 1927 and vol. 18 (1), Chicago, 1928.

Freuchen, Peter, *Arctic Adventure*. Farrar & Rinehart, New York, 1935.

Freuchen, Peter and Salomonsen, Finn, *The Arctic Year*. Jonathan Cape Ltd., London, 1959.

Freuchen, Peter, *Book of the Eskimos*. The World Publishing Co., Cleveland & New York, 1961.

Freuchen, Peter, *Field Notes and Biological Observations*. Mammals: Part II Report of the Fifth Thule Expedition, vol. II, no. 4-5, Copenhagen, 1935.

Gad, Finn, *The History of Greenland, Vol. I, From Earliest Times to 1700*. Translated by Ernst Dupont. McGill-Queen's University Press, 1971.

Gilberg, Rolf, *Changes in the Life of the Polar Eskimos Resulting from a Canadian Immigration into the Thule District, North Greenland, in the 1860s*. Folk, vol. 16/17, Copenhagen, 1974/ 1975.

Gilberg, Rolf, *The Polar Eskimo Population, Thule District, North Greenland*. Meddelelser om Grønland, bd. 203, no. 3, Copenhagen, 1976.

Graburn, N.H., and Strong, B.S., *Circumpolar Peoples: An Anthropological Perspective*. Goodyear Regional Anthropology Series, Pacific Palisades, California, 1973.

Hansen, Keld, *The People of the Far North*. Folk, vol. 11/12, Copenhagen, 1969/1970.

Hayes, Dr. I.I., *The Open Polar Sea*: Sampson, Low, Son & Marston, London, 1867.

Herbert, Marie, *The Snow People*. Barrie & Jenkins, London, 1973.

Herbert, Wally, *Eskimos*. Collins International Library, Glasgow, 1971.

Herbert, Wally, *Polar Deserts*. Collins International Library, Glasgow, 1971.

Holtved, Erik, *Archaeological Investigations in the Thule District*. Meddelelser om Grønland, 3 vols., bd. 141, nos. 1 and 2; bd. 146, no. 3, Copenhagen, 1944-1954.

Holtved, Erik, *Contribution to Polar Eskimo Ethnography*. Meddelelser om Grønland, bd. 182, no. 2, Copenhagen, 1967.

Holtved, Erik, *The Polar Eskimos; Language and Folklore*. Meddelelser om Grønland, 2 vols., bd. 152, nos. 1 and 2, Copenhagen, 1951.

Hrdlicka, Ales, *Contribution to the Anthropology of Central and Smith Sound Eskimo*. Anthropological Papers of the American Museum of Natural History, vol. V, pt. II, New York, 1910.

Hughes, C.C., *Eskimo Boyhood*. The University Press of Kentucky, 1974.

Jensen, Bent, *Folkways of Greenland Dog-Keeping*. Folk, vol. 3, Copenhagen, 1961.

Kane, Elisha, Kent, *Arctic Explorations in the Years 1853, '54, '55*. 2 vols., Childs & Peterson, London, Philadelphia, 1856.

Kjellstrom, Rolf, *Senilicide and Invalidicide among the Eskimos*. Folk, vol. 16/17, Copenhagen, 1974/1975.

Kleivan, Helge, *Culture and Ethnic Identity: On Modernization and Ethnicity in Greenland*. Folk, vol. 11/12, Copenhagen, 1969/1970.

Kleivan, Helge, *Language and Ethnic Identity: Language Policy and Debate in Greenland*. Folk, vol. 11/12, Copenhagen, 1969/1970.

Kleivan, Inge, *Examples of Greenlandic Humour with Regard to Culture Contacts and Inter-Ethnic Relationships*. Folk, vol. 16/17, Copenhagen, 1974/ 1975.

Knuth, Eigil, *The Independence II Bone Artifacts and the Dorset-Evidence in North Greenland*. Folk, vol. 10, Copenhagen, 1968.

Knuth, Eigil, *The "Old Nûgdlît Culture" Site at Nûgdlît Peninsula, Thule District, and the "Mesoeskimo" Site below it*. Folk, vol. 19/20, Copenhagen, 1977/ 1978.

Kroeber, A.L., *The Eskimo of Smith Sound*. Bulletin of American Museum of Natural History, no. 12, New York, 1899.

Lisitzky, Genevieve Helen, *Four Ways of Being Human*. Dennis Dobson, London, 1963.

Malaurie, Jean Noel, *The Last Kings of Thule*. Translated by G. Freeman. George Allen & Unwin Ltd., London, 1956.

Markham, C. R., *The Arctic Highlanders*. Ethnological Society of London, Transactions, no. 4, London, 1866.

McGhee, Robert, *Speculations on Climatic Change and Thule Culture Development*. Folk, vol. 11/12, Copenhagen, 1969/1970.

Ministeriet for Grønland, *Grønland 1978*.

Mirsky, Jeanette, *To the Arctic!* Allan Wingate Limited, London & New York, 1949.

Oswalt, Wendel H., *Eskimos and Explorers*. Chandler & Sharp, Novato, California, 1978.

Peary, Robert E., *Nearest the Pole*. Hutchinson & Co., London, 1907.

Peary, Robert E., *The North Pole*. Hodder & Stoughton, London, 1910.

Peary, Robert E., *Northward Over the "Great Ice"*. 2 vols., Methuen & Co., London, 1898.

Petersen, Robert, *The Greenland Tupilak*. Folk, vol. 4, Copenhagen, 1962.

Petersen, Robert, *The Last Eskimo Immigration into Greenland*. Folk, vol. 4, Copenhagen, 1962.

Rasmussen, Knud, *Greenland by the Polar Sea*. Translated by Asta and Rowland Kenney. William Heinemann, London, 1921.

Rasmussen, Knud, *The People of the Polar North*. Compiled from the Danish originals and edited by G. Herring. Kegan Paul, Trench, Trübner & Co. Ltd., London, 1908.

Rink, H. J., *Tales and Traditions of the Eskimos*. Edited by R. Brown. William Blackwood & Sons, London & Edinburgh, 1875.

Ross, Captain John, *A Voyage of Discovery in H.M. Ships "Isabella" and "Alexander"*. John Murray, London, 1819.

Søby, Regitze Margrethe, *The Kinship Terminology in Thule*. Folk, vol. 19/20, Copenhagen, 1977/1978.

Steensby, H. P., *Contribution to the Ethnology and Anthropogeography of the Polar Eskimos*. Meddelelser om Grønland, bd. 34, no. 7, Copenhagen, 1910.

Stone, James W. Van, *The First Peary Collection of Polar Eskimo Material Culture*. Fieldiana Anthropology, vol. 36, no. 2, Field Museum of Natural History, Chicago, 1972.

Thorén, R., *Picture Atlas of the Arctic*. Elsevier Publishing Co., Amsterdam, 1969.

Walker, Ernest P., *Mammals of the World*. 2 vols., John Hopkins Press, Baltimore, 1964.

Acknowledgements and Picture Credits

The author and editors of this book wish to thank the following: Cherry Alexander; Dr. Robert Bud, The Science Museum, London; Franklin W. Burch (Director), Gerald Pagano, Alison Wilson, National Archives' Center for Polar and Scientific Archives, Washington, D.C.; N. O. Christensen, Director, Arktisk Institut, Charlottenland; John Cole; Katrina van Duyn; Hans Engelund; Jens Fynbo (Director), Royal Greenland Trade Department, Copenhagen; Marie Herbert; Eigil Jensen; Rasmus Lau; Ministeriet for Grønland, Copenhagen; Marilyn Murphy; Library of the Museum of Mankind, London; Kathy Nolan; Simon Rigge; John Roberts; Royal Danish Embassy, London; Library of the Royal Geographical Society, London; Adrian Saunders; Michael Schwab; Roy Vickery, Department of Botany, British Museum (Natural History); Lucy Voulgaris; Library of the Zoological Society, London.

The sources for the pictures in this book are listed below. Credits for each of the photographers and illustrators are listed by page number in sequence; where necessary, the locations of pictures within pages are also indicated—separated from page numbers by dashes.

All photographs by Bryan Alexander except: Cherry Alexander, 4—bottom, 10, 13, 17, 38-39, 64, 135—top right and left, middle right and bottom left, 137—bottom, 152-153. Fred Breummer, cover portrait, 9, 11, 36-37, 133. Frank Herrmann, *Sunday Times*, 4—top. National Archives, Washington, D.C., James Davidson Papers (RG 401), 93, 94—top, 95. National Archives, Washington, D.C., Peary Family Collection (RG 401), 94— bottom. The Scott Polar Research Institute, 26-27.

Illustrations (alphabetically): Maps by Terry Allen and Nicholas Skelton for Creative Cartography Ltd., 20-21, 23, 108. Front endpaper map by Engineering Surveys Reproduction Ltd. Grundy and Northedge Designers, 100-101.

Index

Numerals in italics indicate an illustration.

L

M

N

O

P

Q

R

S

T

V

W

Colour separations by Scan Studios Ltd.—Dublin, Ireland.
Typesetting by G. Beard & Son, Ltd.—Brighton, England.
Printed and bound by Brepols S.A.—Turnhout, Belgium.